Life in Classrooms

PHILIP W. JACKSON
UNIVERSITY OF CHICAGO

But to go to school on a summer morn,
O, it drives all joy away;
Under a cruel eye outworn,
The little ones spend the day
In sighing and dismay.

William Blake

Holt, Rinehart and Winston, Inc.

New York • Chicago • San Francisco • Atlanta
Dallas • Toronto • Montreal • London

1976

he kept

URTEEN DAYS

ed for   he book is kept   ertime.

Life in
Classrooms

To Nancy, David, and Steven

Preface

This book is written for all who are interested in schools and children, but most especially for teachers, administrators, and others whose daily work brings them into direct contact with classroom life. Its aim is neither to damn schools nor to praise them, nor even, necessarily, to change them. Rather, the goal is simply to arouse the reader's interest and possibly to awaken his concern over aspects of school life that seem to be receiving less attention than they deserve.

The text focuses almost exclusively on what happens in elementary school classrooms. This emphasis on the early years of schooling is quite intentional, for it is during that period that the young child comes to grips with the facts of institutional life. Also during these formative years he develops adaptive strategies that will stay with him throughout the balance of his education and beyond. Life in high school and college classrooms is surely different from life in the lower grades, but beneath the obvious differences there lies a basic similarity. In a fundamental sense, school is school, no matter where it happens.

Stylistically, the book is a mélange. Descriptions of empirical studies are interlaced with speculative asides; tabular materials sometimes share the page with the most unquantifiable assertions. The expository tone is hard in some sections, and soft in others. But this mixture is not without purpose. Classroom life, in my judgment, is too complex an affair to be viewed or talked about from any single perspective. Accordingly, as we try to grasp the meaning of what school is like for students and teachers we must not hesitate to use all the ways of knowing at our disposal. This means we must read, and look, and listen, and count things, and talk to people, and even muse introspectively over the memories of our own childhood. Ultimately, of course we are tempted to write about what we know. In this book I have tried to blend these varied approaches to my subject.

Several of the studies on which I have drawn, and particularly those discussed in Chapters II and III, may seem curiously out-of-date to some readers. In these days of massive research support and electronic data processing, new findings are tumbling off the press almost faster than they can be consumed by a research-hungry public. It may seem strange that I have dusted off and presented for serious consideration the findings of investigators whose work, by today's standards, would hardly pass muster in an undergraduate course on research design. But several of these early studies are surprisingly informative about important matters that are not presently being examined by researchers. Today's reader should not lay aside his critical faculties when examining these early investigations, but neither should his interest in the new and the timely prevent him from making good use of yesterday's labors.

This is not a textbook and, therefore, it does not contain a systematic, or even an unsystematic, review of the many extant studies of classroom phenomena. The reader who is seeking an overview of the interesting research done by Marie Hughes, B. O. Smith, Arno Bellack, Jacob Kounin, Bruce Biddle, Louis Smith, Edmund Amidon, Ned Flanders, and others, will not find it here. Indeed, even the names of these prominent investigators are barely mentioned in the pages that follow. This omission is not an oversight but is a necessity in a book that tries to focus on some of the unexplored terrain in an increasingly well-traveled field.

The point of view expounded here had its beginning in 1962 while I was a Fellow at the Center for Advanced Study in the Behavioral Sciences. During that year I visited a small number of elementary school classrooms in Palo Alto, California. Those visits convinced me of the value of moving up close to the social realities of school life. I am grateful to Francis S. Chase, who was then Chairman of the Department of Education at the University of Chicago, for making my stay at the Center possible and to Ralph Tyler and his staff for creating an environment in which I was encouraged to move off in new directions. Special thanks are due Margaret Allison, Joyce Bryson, and Lloyd Busher, the three teachers who permitted me to sit quietly in the back of their classroom throughout much of that year and who patiently endured my questioning during their lunch hours and coffee breaks.

When I returned to Chicago in the Fall of 1963 I decided to continue making systematic classroom observations and with the cooperation of Robert Newman, then principal of the Lower School of the University of Chicago Laboratory School, I gained entrance to two fourth-grade rooms under the direction of Fay Abrams and Louise Pliss. Later I extended my "sample" to include the first-grade class taught by Judith Jones and the second-grade class taught by Heather Carter. My many visits to those four classrooms and my frequent conversations with the teachers provided the raw materal for several of the ideas contained herein. Most teachers can tolerate an occasional visitor without difficulty, but when the visitor returns day after day for a period of two years and when he insists on staying after school and on following the teacher to the teacher's lounge and to the playground, it would be understandable if his welcome began to wear a bit thin. I can only say that if these four Laboratory School teachers ever possessed such feelings about my visits they artfully disguised them in my presence. The fact that I developed and maintained a close friendship with each of them is testimony to their pedagogical fortitude. Every classroom observer should be so fortunate.

Various drafts of the manuscript were read by Henriette Lahaderne, Bernice Wolfson, Lawrence Kohlberg, Bruce Biddle, and Dale Harris. I am grateful to them for their encouragement, their frank criticism, and their wise counsel. Although I accept full responsibility for any defects the book might have, credit for its strengths, such as they are, must be shared with these perceptive readers. I wish to acknowledge the help of my secretary, Yvette Courtade, who skillfully deciphered my illegible handwriting and typed the first complete draft of the manuscript.

Portions of this book have appeared in articles in *The School Review, Elementary School Journal,* and the *Journal of Educational Psychology.* I am grateful to the publishers of those journals for granting me permission to use this material.

As each small piece of the writing was completed I often would ask my wife, Jo, to react to what I had written. I learned to rely heavily on her sensitivity to unclear passages and other rough spots in the manuscript. More important than her editorial acumen, however, was her faith in this project, a faith which she somehow communicated without ever putting it into words.

Chicago, Illinois   P. W. J.
January, 1968

Contents

xi

Life in
Classrooms

The Daily Grind 1

The "order," the trivia of the institution is, in human terms, a disorder, and as such, must be resisted. It's truly a sign of psychic health that the young are already aware of this.

Theodore Roethke, *On the Poet and His Craft*

On a typical weekday morning between September and June some 35 million Americans kiss their loved ones goodby, pick up their lunch pails and books, and leave to spend their day in that collection of enclosures (totalling about one million) known as elementary school classrooms. This massive exodus from home to school is accomplished with a minimum of fuss and bother. Few tears are shed (except perhaps by the very youngest) and few cheers are raised. The school attendance of children is such a common experience in our society that those of us who watch them go hardly pause to consider what happens to them when they get there. Of course our indifference disappears occasionally. When something goes wrong or when we have been notified of his remarkable achievement, we might ponder, for a moment at least, the meaning of the experience for the child in question, but most of the time we simply note that our Johnny is on his way to school, and now, it is time for our second cup of coffee.

Parents are interested, to be sure, in how *well* Johnny does while there, and when he comes trudging home they may ask him questions about what happened today or, more generally, how things went. But both their questions and his answers typically focus on the highlights of the school experience—its unusual aspects—rather than on the mundane and seemingly trivial events that filled the bulk of his school hours. Parents are interested, in other words, in the spice of school life rather than in its substance.

Teachers, too, are chiefly concerned with only a very narrow aspect of a youngster's school experience. They, too, are likely to focus on specific acts of misbehavior or accomplishment as representing what a particular student did in school today, even though the acts in question occupied but a small fraction of the student's time. Teachers, like parents, seldom ponder the significance of the thousands of fleeting events that combine to form the routine of the classroom.

And the student himself is no less selective. Even if someone bothered to question him about the minutiae of his school day, he would probably be unable to give a complete account of what he had done. For him, too, the day has been reduced in memory into a small number of signal events—"I got 100 on my spelling test,"

"A new boy came and he sat next to me."—or recurring activities—
"We went to gym," "We had music." His spontaneous recall of detail
is not much greater than that required to answer our conventional
questions.

This concentration on the highlights of school life is understandable from the standpoint of human interest. A similar selection
process operates when we inquire into or recount other types of
daily activity. When we are asked about our trip downtown or our
day at the office we rarely bother describing the ride on the bus or
the time spent in front of the watercooler. Indeed, we are more
likely to report that nothing happened than to catalogue the
pedestrian actions that took place between home and return. Unless
something interesting occurred there is little purpose in talking
about our experience.

Yet from the standpoint of giving shape and meaning to our
lives these events about which we rarely speak may be as important
as those that hold our listener's attention. Certainly they represent
a much larger portion of our experience than do those about which
we talk. The daily routine, the "rat race," and the infamous "old
grind" may be brightened from time to time by happenings that add
color to an otherwise drab existence, but the grayness of our daily
lives has an abrasive potency of its own. Anthropologists understand this fact better than do most other social scientists, and their
field studies have taught us to appreciate the cultural significance
of the humdrum elements of human existence. This is the lesson we
must heed as we seek to understand life in elementary classrooms.

I

School is a place where tests are failed and passed, where amusing
things happen, where new insights are stumbled upon, and skills
acquired. But it is also a place in which people sit, and listen, and
wait, and raise their hands, and pass out paper, and stand in line,
and sharpen pencils. School is where we encounter both friends and
foes, where imagination is unleashed and misunderstanding brought
to ground. But it is also a place in which yawns are stifled and
initials scratched on desktops, where milk money is collected and
recess lines are formed. Both aspects of school life, the celebrated
and the unnoticed, are familiar to all of us, but the latter, if only
because of its characteristic neglect, seems to deserve more attention
than it has received to date from those who are interested in
education.

In order to appreciate the significance of trivial classroom events it is necessary to consider the frequency of their occurrence, the standardization of the school environment, and the compulsory quality of daily attendence. We must recognize, in other words, that children are in school for a long time, that the settings in which they perform are highly uniform, and that they are there whether they want to be or not. Each of these three facts, although seemingly obvious, deserves some elaboration, for each contributes to our understanding of how students feel about and cope with their school experience.

The amount of time children spend in school can be described with a fair amount of quantitative precision, although the psychological significance of the numbers involved is another matter entirely. In most states the school year legally comprises 180 days. A full session on each of those days usually lasts about six hours (with a break for lunch), beginning somewhere around nine o'clock in the morning and ending about three o'clock in the afternoon. Thus, if a student never misses a day during the year, he spends a little more than one thousand hours under the care and tutelage of teachers. If he has attended kindergarten and was reasonably regular in his attendance during the grades, he will have logged a little more than seven thousand classroom hours by the time he is ready for junior high school.

The magnitude of 7000 hours spread over six or seven years of a child's life is difficult to comprehend. On the one hand, when placed beside the total number of hours the child has lived during those years it is not very great—slightly more than one-tenth of his life during the time in question, about one-third of his hours of sleep during that period. On the other hand, aside from sleeping, and perhaps playing, there is no other activity that occupies as much of the child's time as that involved in attending school. Apart from the bedroom (where he has his eyes closed most of the time) there is no single enclosure in which he spends a longer time than he does in the classroom. From the age of six onward he is a more familiar sight to his teacher than to his father, and possibly even to his mother.

Another way of estimating what all those hours in the classroom mean is to ask how long it would take to accumulate them while engaged in some other familiar and recurring activity. Church attendance provides an interesting comparison. In order to have had as much time in church as a sixth grader has had in classrooms we would have to spend all day at a religious gathering every Sunday for more than 24 years. Or, if we prefer our devotion in smaller doses, we would have to attend a one-hour service every Sunday for 150 years before the inside of a church became as familiar to us as the inside of a school is to a twelve-year-old.

The comparison with church attendance is dramatic, and perhaps overly so. But it does make us stop and think about the possible significance of an otherwise meaningless number. Also, aside from the home and the school there is no physical setting in which people of all ages congregate with as great a regularity as they do in church.

The translation of the child's tenure in class into terms of weekly church attendance serves a further purpose. It sets the stage for considering an important similarity between the two institutions: school and church. The inhabitants of both are surrounded by a stable and highly stylized environment. The fact of prolonged exposure in either setting increases in its meaning as we begin to consider the elements of repetition, redundancy, and ritualistic action that are experienced there.

A classroom, like a church auditorium, is rarely seen as being anything other than that which it is. No one entering either place is likely to think that he is in a living room, or a grocery store, or a train station. Even if he entered at midnight or at some other time when the activities of the people would not give the function away, he would have no difficulty understanding what was *supposed* to go on there. Even devoid of people, a church is a church and a classroom, a classroom.

This is not to say, of course, that all classrooms are identical, anymore than all churches are. Clearly there are differences, and sometimes very extreme ones, between any two settings. One has only to think of the wooden benches and planked floor of the early American classroom as compared with the plastic chairs and tile flooring in today's suburban schools. But the resemblance is still there despite the differences, and, more important, during any particular historical period the differences are not that great. Also, whether the student moves from first to sixth grade on floors of vinyl tile or oiled wood, whether he spends his days in front of a black blackboard or a green one, is not as important as the fact that the environment in which he spends these six or seven years is highly stable.

In their efforts to make their classrooms more homelike, elementary school teachers often spend considerable time fussing with the room's decorations. Bulletin boards are changed, new pictures are hung, and the seating arrangement is altered from circles to rows and back again. But these are surface adjustments at best, resembling the work of the inspired housewife who rearranges the living room furniture and changes the color of the drapes in order to make the room more "interesting." School bulletin boards may be changed but they are never discarded, the seats may be rearranged but thirty of them are there to stay, the teacher's desk may have a new plant on it but there it sits, as ubiquitous as the roll-down maps, the olive drab wastebasket, and the pencil sharpener on the window ledge.

Even the odors of the classroom are fairly standardized. Schools may use different brands of wax and cleaning fluid, but they all seem to contain similar ingredients, a sort of universal smell which creates an aromatic background that permeates the entire building. Added to this, in each classroom, is the slightly acrid scent of chalk dust and the faint hint of fresh wood from the pencil shavings. In some rooms, especially at lunch time, there is the familiar odor of orange peels and peanut butter sandwiches, a blend that mingles in the late afternoon (following recess) with the delicate pungency of children's perspiration. If a person stumbled into a classroom blindfolded, his nose alone, if he used it carefully, would tell him where he was.

All of these sights and smells become so familiar to students and teachers alike that they exist dimly, on the periphery of awareness. Only when the classroom is encountered under somewhat unusual circumstances, does it appear, for a moment, a strange place filled with objects that command our attention. On these rare occasions when, for example, students return to school in the evening, or in the summer when the halls ring with the hammers of workmen, many features of the school environment that have merged into an undifferentiated background for its daily inhabitants suddenly stand out in sharp relief. This experience, which obviously occurs in contexts other than the classroom, can only happen in settings to which the viewer has become uncommonly habituated.

Not only is the classroom a relatively stable physical environment, it also provides a fairly constant social context. Behind the same old desks sit the same old students, in front of the familiar blackboard stands the familiar teacher. There are changes, to be sure,—some students come and go during the year and on a few mornings the children are greeted at the door by a strange adult. But in most cases these events are sufficiently uncommon to create a flurry of excitement in the room. Moreover, in most ele..entary classrooms the social composition is not only stable, it is also physically arranged with considerable regularity. Each student has an assigned seat and, under normal circumstances, that is where he is to be found. The practice of assigning seats makes it possible for the teacher or a student to take attendance at a glance. A quick visual sweep is usually sufficient to determine who is there and who is not. The ease with which this procedure is accomplished reveals more eloquently than do words how accustomed each member of the class is to the presence of every other member.

An additional feature of the social atmosphere of elementary classrooms deserves at least passing comment. There is a social intimacy in schools that is unmatched elsewhere in our society. Buses and movie theaters may be more crowded than classrooms, but people rarely stay in such densely populated settings for extended periods of time and while there, they usually are not expected to concentrate on work or to interact with each other. Even factory workers are not clustered as close together as students in a standard classroom. Indeed, imagine what would happen if a factory the size of a typical elementary school contained three or four hundred adult workers. In all likelihood the unions would not allow it. Only in schools do thirty or more people spend several hours each day literally side by side. Once we leave the classroom we seldom again are required to have contact with so many people for so long a time. This fact will become particularly relevant in a later chapter in which we treat the social demands of life in school.

A final aspect of the constancy experienced by young students involves the ritualistic and cyclic quality of the activities carried on in the classroom. The daily schedule, as an instance, is commonly divided into definite periods during which specific subjects are to be studied or specific activities engaged in. The content of the work surely changes from day to day and from week to week, and in this sense there is considerable variety amid the constancy. But spelling still comes after arithmetic on Tuesday morning, and when the teacher says, "All right class, now take out your spellers," his announcement comes as no surprise to the students. Further, as they search in their desks for their spelling textbooks, the children may not know what new words will be included in the day's assignment, but they have a fairly clear idea of what the next twenty minutes of class time will entail.

Despite the diversity of subject matter content, the identifiable forms of classroom activity are not great in number. The labels: "seatwork," "group discussion," "teacher demonstration," and "question-and-answer period" (which would include work "at the board"), are sufficient to categorize most of the things that happen when class is in session. "Audio-visual display," "testing session," and "games" might be added to the list, but in most elementary classrooms they occur rarely.

Each of these major activities are performed according to rather well-defined rules which the students are expected to understand and obey—for example, no loud talking during seatwork, do not interrupt someone else during discussion, keep your eyes on your own paper during tests, raise your hand if you have a question. Even in the early grades these rules are so well understood by the students (if not completely internalized) that the teacher has only to give very abbreviated signals ("Voices, class." "Hands, please.")

when violations are perceived. In many classrooms a weekly time schedule is permanently posted so that everyone can tell at a glance what will happen next.

Thus, when our young student enters school in the morning he is entering an environment with which he has become exceptionally familiar through prolonged exposure. Moreover, it is a fairly stable environment—one in which the physical objects, social relations, and major activities remain much the same from day to day, week to week, and even, in certain respects, from year to year. Life there resembles life in other contexts in some ways, but not all. There is, in other words, a uniqueness to the student's world. School, like church and home, is someplace special. Look where you may, you will not find another place quite like it

There is an important fact about a student's life that teachers and parents often prefer not to talk about, at least not in front of students. This is the fact that young people have to be in school, whether they want to be or not. In this regard students have something in common with the members of two other of our social institutions that have involuntary attendance: prisons and mental hospitals. The analogy, though dramatic, is not intended to be shocking, and certainly there is no comparison between the unpleasantness of life for inmates of our prisons and mental institutions, on the one hand, and the daily travails of a first or second grader, on the other. Yet the school child, like the incarcerated adult, is, in a sense, a prisoner. He too must come to grips with the inevitability of his experience. He too must develop strategies for dealing with the conflict that frequently arises between his natural desires and interests on the one hand and institutional expectations on the other. Several of these strategies will be discussed in the chapters that follow. Here it is sufficient to note that the thousands of hours spent in the highly stylized environment of the elementary classroom are not, in an ultimate sense, a matter of choice, even though some children might prefer school to play. Many seven-year-olds skip happily to school, and as parents and teachers we are glad they do, but we stand ready to enforce the attendance of those who are more reluctant. And our vigilance does not go unnoticed by children.

In sum, classrooms are special places. The things that happen there and the ways in which they happen combine to make these settings different from all others. This is not to say, of course, that there is no similarity between what goes on in school and the students' experiences elsewhere. Classrooms are indeed like homes and churches and hospital wards in many important respects. But not in all.

The things that make schools different from other places are not only the paraphernalia of learning and teaching and the educational content of the dialogues that take place there, although these are the features that are usually singled out when we try to portray what life in school is really like. It is true that nowhere else do we find blackboards and teachers and textbooks in such abundance and nowhere else is so much time spent on reading, writing, and arithmetic. But these obvious characteristics do not constitute all that is unique about this environment. There are other features, much less obvious though equally omnipresent, that help to make up "the facts of life," as it were, to which students must adapt. From the standpoint of understanding the impact of school life on the student some features of the classroom that are not immediately visible are fully as important as those that are.

The characteristics of school life to which we now turn our attention are not commonly mentioned by students, at least not directly, nor are they apparent to the casual observer. Yet they are as real, in a sense, as the unfinished portrait of Washington that hangs above the cloakroom door. They comprise three facts of life with which even the youngest student must learn to deal and may be introduced by the key words: *crowds, praise,* and *power.*

Learning to live in a classroom involves, among other things, learning to live in a crowd. This simple truth has already been mentioned, but it requires greater elaboration. Most of the things that are done in school are done with others, or at least in the presence of others, and this fact has profound implications for determining the quality of a student's life.

Of equal importance is the fact that schools are basically evaluative settings. The very young student may be temporarily fooled by tests that are presented as games, but it doesn't take long before he begins to see through the subterfuge and comes to realize that school, after all, is a serious business. It is not only what you do there but what others think of what you do that is important. Adaptation to school life requires the student to become used to living under the constant condition of having his words and deeds evaluated by others.

School is also a place in which the division between the weak and the powerful is clearly drawn. This may sound like a harsh way to describe the separation between teachers and students, but it serves to emphasize a fact that is often overlooked, or touched upon gingerly at best. Teachers are indeed more powerful than students, in the sense of having greater responsibility for giving shape to classroom events, and this sharp difference in authority is another feature of school life with which students must learn how to deal.

In three major ways then—as members of crowds, as potential recipients of praise or reproof, and as pawns of institutional authorities—students are confronted with aspects of reality that at least during their childhood years are relatively confined to the hours spent in classrooms. Admittedly, similar conditions are encountered in other environments. Students, when they are not performing as such, must often find themselves lodged within larger groups, serving as targets of praise or reproof, and being bossed around or guided by persons in positions of higher authority. But these kinds of experiences are particularly frequent while school is in session and it is likely during this time that adaptive strategies having relevance for other contexts and other life periods are developed.

In the sections of this chapter to follow, each of the three classroom qualities that have been briefly mentioned will be described in greater detail. Particular emphasis will be given to the manner in which students cope with these aspects of their daily lives. The goal of this discussion, as in the preceding chapters, is to deepen our understanding of the peculiar mark that school life makes on us all.

II

Anyone who has ever taught knows that the classroom is a busy place, even though it may not always appear so to the casual visitor. Indeed, recent data have proved surprising even to experienced teachers. For example, we have found in one study of elementary classrooms that the teacher engages in as many as 1000 interpersonal interchanges each day.[1] An attempt to catalogue the interchanges among students or the physical movement of class members would doubtlessly add to the general impression that most classrooms, though seemingly placid when glimpsed through the window in the hall door, are more like the proverbial beehive of activity. One way of understanding the meaning of this activity for those who experience it is by focusing on the teacher as he goes about channeling the social traffic of the classroom.

First, consider the rapidity of the teacher's actions. What keeps him hopping from Jane to Billy to Sam, and back again, in the space of a few seconds? Clearly much of this activity is done in the interest of instruction. Teaching commonly involves talking and the teacher acts as a gatekeeper who manages the flow of the classroom dialogue. When a student wishes to say something during a discussion it is usually the teacher's job to recognize his wish and

---

[1] Philip W. Jackson, "Teacher-pupil communication in the elementary classroom: an observational study," Paper read at the American Educational Research Association meeting, Chicago, February 1965.

to invite his comment. When more than one person wishes to enter the discussion or answer a question at the same time (a most common event) it is the teacher who decides who will speak and in what order. Or we might turn the observation around and say that the teacher determines who will *not* speak, for when a group of students have signalled the desire to enter the dialogue, several of them may be planning to say the same thing. Therefore, if Johnny is called on first, Billy, who also had his hand raised, may now find himself without anything to say. This fact partially explains the urgency with which the desire to speak is signalled to the teacher.

Another time-consuming task for the teacher, at least in the elementary school, is that of serving as supply sergeant. Classroom space and material resources are limited and the teacher must allocate these resources judiciously. Only one student at a time can borrow the big scissors, or look through the microscope, or drink from the drinking fountain, or use the pencil sharpener. And broken pencil points and parched throats obviously do not develop one at a time or in an orderly fashion. Therefore, the number of students desiring to use various classroom resources at any given moment is often greater than the number that can use them. This explains the lines of students that form in front of the pencil sharpener, the drinking fountain, the microscope, and the washroom door.

Closely related to the job of doling out material resources is that of granting special privileges to deserving students. In elementary classrooms it is usually the teacher who assigns coveted duties, such as serving on the safety patrol, or running the movie projector, or clapping the erasers, or handing out supplies. In most classrooms volunteers are plentiful, thus the jobs are often rotated among the students. (A list of current job-holders is a familiar item on elementary school bulletin boards.) Although the delegation of these duties may not take up much of the teacher's time, it does help to give structure to the activities of the room and to fashion the quality of the total experience for many of the participants.

A fourth responsibility of the teacher and one that calls our attention to another important aspect of classroom life, is that of serving as an official timekeeper. It is he who sees to it that things begin and end on time, more or less. He determines the proper moment for switching from discussion to workbooks, or from spelling to arithmetic. He decides whether a student has spent too long in the washroom, or whether those who take the bus may be dismissed. In many schools he is assisted in this job by elaborate systems of bells and buzzers. But even when the school day is mechanically punctuated by clangs and hums, the teacher is not entirely relieved of his responsibility for watching the clock. The implications of the teacher clock-watching behavior for determining what life in school is like are indeed profound. This behavior reminds us, above all, that school is a place where things often happen not because students want them to, but because it is time for them to occur.

All of the teacher's actions described so far are bound together by a common theme. They are all responsive, in one way or another, to the crowded condition of the classroom. If the teacher dealt with one student at a time (as does happen in tutorial settings) most of the tasks that have been mentioned would be unnecessary. It is, in part, the press of numbers and of time that keeps the teacher so busy. But our ultimate concern, it must be remembered, is with the student and the quality of *his* life in the classroom. Therefore, the frenetic activity of the teacher as he goes about calling on students, handing out supplies, granting privileges, and turning activities on and off, is of interest, within the present context, only insofar as that behavior tells us something about what school is like for those who are at the receiving end of the teacher's action.

The things the teacher does as he works within the physical, temporal, and social limits of the classroom have a constraining effect upon the events that might occur there if individual impulse were allowed free reign. If everyone who so desired tried to speak at once, or struggled for possession of the big scissors, or offered a helping hand in threading the movie projector, classroom life would be much more hectic than it commonly is. If students were allowed to stick with a subject until they grew tired of it on their own, our present curriculum would have to be modified drastically. Obviously, some kinds of controls are necessary if the school's goals are to be reached and social chaos averted. The question of whether the teacher should or should not serve as a combination traffic cop, judge, supply sergeant, and time-keeper is somewhat irrelevant to the present discussion, but the fact that such functions must be performed, even if the responsibility for performing them falls upon individual students, is far from irrelevant. For a world in which traffic signs, whistles, and other regulatory devices abound is quite different from one in which these features are absent.

One of the inevitable outcomes of traffic management is the experiencing of delay. In crowded situations where people are forced to take turns in using limited resources, some must stand by until others have finished. When people are required to move as a group toward a goal, the speed of the group is, necessarily, the speed of its slowest member. Almost inevitably, therefore, in such situations some group members are waiting for the others to catch up. Moreover, whenever the future is thought to be more attractive than the present—a common perception among school children—slow movement can sometimes seem like no movement at all.

All of these different kinds of delay are commonplace in the classrooms. Indeed, when we begin to examine the details of classroom life carefully, it is surprising to see how much of the students' time is spent in waiting. The most obvious examples are to be found in the practice of lining up that has already been mentioned. In most elementary schools students stand in line several times a day. The entire class typically lines up during recess, lunch, and dismissal, and then there are the smaller lines that form sporadically in front of drinking fountains, pencil sharpeners, and the like. Furthermore, it is not uncommon for teachers to hold these lines motionless until talking has ceased and some semblance of uniformity and order has been achieved.

Nor does the waiting end when the line has disappeared. Even when students are sitting in their seats they are often in the same position, psychologically, as if they were members of a line. It is not uncommon, for example, for teachers to move down rows asking questions or calling for recitations or examining seatwork. Under these conditions students interact with the teacher in a fixed order with the consequence of each student waiting until his turn arrives, speaking his piece, and then waiting for the teacher to get to him again in the next round. Even in rooms where teachers do not operate "by the numbers," as it were, the idea of taking turns during discussion and recitation periods is still present. After a student has made a contribution in a more informally run class the teacher is less likely to call on him again, at least for a brief period of time. Conversely, a student who has said nothing all period is more likely to have his raised hand recognized than is a student who has participated several times in the lesson. Unusual variations from this procedure would be considered unfair by students and teachers alike. Thus, even during so-called free discussion invisible lines are formed.

In rooms where students have considerable freedom to move about on their own during seatwork and study periods, the teacher himself often becomes the center of little groups of waiting students. One of the most typical social arrangements in such settings is that in which the teacher is chatting with one student or examining his work while two or three others stand by, books and papers in hand, waiting to have the teacher evaluate their work, give them further direction, answer their questions, or in some other fashion enable them to move along. At such moments it is not unusual for one or two of the seated students also to have their hands raised, propped at the elbow, waiting patiently for the teacher to get around to them.

A familiar arrangement in the lower grades is for the teacher to work with a part of the class, usually a reading group, while the remainder engage in seatwork. Not uncommonly the students working by themselves finish their assignments before the teacher is finished with the group with which he is working. Under such circumstances it is not uncommon for the teacher to admonish the students to "find something to do" until it is time for a new activity to begin. These students may obey the teacher and thus appear to be busy, but their busyness is analogous to that of patients who read the old magazines in the doctor's waiting room.

A final example of the kinds of delay to be observed in the classroom involves the situation in which the group is given a problem to solve or an exercise to complete and some students complete the work long before others. At such times the teacher may be heard to ask, "How many need more time?" or to command, "Raise your hand when you have finished." This type of delay may only last a few seconds, but it occurs very frequently in some classrooms. Further, it is a kind of delay that is not experienced equally by all students, as are some of the others that have been mentioned, but tends, instead, to be encountered most frequently by students who are brighter, or faster, or more involved in their work.

Thus, in several different ways students in elementary classrooms are required to wait their turn and to delay their actions. No one knows for certain how much of the average student's time is spent in neutral, as it were, but for many students in many classrooms it must be a memorable portion. Furthermore, delay is only one of the consequences of living in a crowd and perhaps not even the most important one from the standpoint of constraining the individual. Waiting is not so bad, and may even be beneficial, when the things we are waiting for come to pass. But waiting, as we all know, can sometimes be in vain.

The denial of desire is the ultimate outcome of many of the delays occurring in the classroom. The raised hand is sometimes ignored, the question to the teacher is sometimes brushed aside, the permission that is sought is sometimes refused. No doubt things often have to be this way. Not everyone who wants to speak can be heard, not all of the student's queries can be answered to his satisfaction, not all of their requests can be granted. Also, it is probably true that most of these denials are psychologically trivial when considered individually. But when considered cumulatively their significance increases. And regardless of whether or not they are justified, they make it clear that part of learning how to live in school involves learning how to give up desire as well as how to wait for its fulfillment.

Interruptions of many sorts create a third feature of classroom life that results, at least in part, from the crowded social conditions. During group sessions irrelevant comments, misbehavior, and outside visitors bearing messages often disrupt the continuity of the lesson. When the teacher is working individually with a student—a common arrangement in elementary classrooms—petty interruptions, usually in the form of other students coming to the teacher for advice, are the rule rather than the exception. Thus. the bubble of reality created during the teaching session is punctured by countless trivial incidents and the teacher must spend time patching up the holes. Students are expected to ignore these distractions or at least to turn quickly back to their studies after their attention has been momentarily drawn elsewhere.

Typically, things happen on time in school and this fact creates interruptions of another sort. Adherence to a time schedule requires that activities often begin before interest is aroused and terminate before interest disappears. Thus students are required to put away their arithmetic book and take out their spellers even though they want to continue with arithmetic and ignore spelling. In the classroom, work is often stopped before it is finished. Questions are often left dangling when the bell rings.

Quite possibly, of course, there is no alternative to this unnatural state of affairs. If teachers were always to wait until students were finished with one activity before they began another, the school day would become interminable. There seems to be no other way, therefore, but to stop and start things by the clock, even though this means constantly interrupting the natural flow of interest and desire for at least some students.

Another aspect of school life, related to the general phenomena of distractions and interruptions, is the recurring demand that the student ignore those who are around him. In elementary classrooms students are frequently assigned seatwork on which they are expected to focus their individual energies. During these seatwork periods talking and other forms of communication between students are discouraged, if not openly forbidden. The general admonition in such situations is to do your own work and leave others alone.

In a sense, then, students must try to behave as if they were in solitude, when in point of fact they are not. They must keep their eyes on their paper when human faces beckon. Indeed, in the early grades it is not uncommon to find students facing each other around a table while at the same time being required not to communicate with each other. These young people, if they are to become successful students, must learn how to be alone in a crowd.

Adults encounter conditions of social solitude so often that they are likely to overlook its special significance in the elementary classroom. We have learned to mind our own business in factories and offices, to remain silent in libraries, and to keep our thoughts to ourselves while riding public conveyances. But there are two major differences between classrooms and most of these other settings. First, except for the first few days of school, a classroom is not an *ad hoc* gathering of strangers. It is a group whose members have come to know each other quite well, to the point of friendship in many cases. Second, attendance in the room is not voluntary, as it is in many other social situations. Students are there whether they want to be or not and the work on which they are expected to concentrate also is often not of their own choosing. Thus, the pull to communicate with others is likely somewhat stronger in the classroom than in other crowded situations.

Here then are four unpublicized features of school life: delay, denial, interruption, and social distraction. Each is produced, in part, by the crowded conditions of the classroom. When twenty or thirty people must live and work together within a limited space for five or six hours a day most of the things that have been discussed are inevitable. Therefore, to decry the existence of these conditions is probably futile, yet their pervasiveness and frequency make them too important to be ignored. One alternative is to study the ways in which teachers and students cope with these facts of life and to seek to discover how that coping might leave its mark on their reactions to the world in general.

First, we must recognize that the severity of the conditions being described is to some extent a function of social tradition, institutional policy, and situational wealth and poverty. In some schools daily schedules are treated casually and in others they are rigidly adhered to. In some classrooms a rule of no talking is in force almost all of the time, while a steady murmur is tolerated in others. In some classrooms there are forty or more students, in others, at the same grade level, there are twenty or less. Some teachers are slow to recognize an upraised hand, others respond almost immediately. Some rooms are equipped with several pairs of big scissors, others have only one.

Despite these differences, however, it is doubtful that there is any classroom in which the phenomena we have been discussing are uncommon. Space, abundant resources, and a liberal attitude toward rules and regulations may reduce the pressure of the crowd somewhat but it certainly does not eliminate it entirely. Indeed, most of the observations on which the present analysis is based were made in so-called advantaged schools whose teachers were proud of their "progressive" educational views.

Second, as we begin to focus on the ways of coping with these institutional demands, it should be recognized at once that adaptive strategies are idiosyncratic to individual students. We cannot predict, in other words, how any particular student will react to the constraints imposed on him in the classroom. We can only identify major adaptive styles that might be used to characterize large numbers of students.

The quintessence of virtue in most institutions is contained in the single word: *patience*. Lacking that quality, life could be miserable for those who must spend their time in our prisons, our factories, our corporation offices, and our schools. In all of these settings the participants must "learn to labour and to wait." They must also, to some extent, learn to suffer in silence. They are expected to bear with equanimity, in other words, the continued delay, denial, and interruption of their personal wishes and desires.

But patience is more of a moral attribute than an adaptive strategy. It is what a person is asked to "be" rather than what he is asked to "do." Moreover, when we consider how a person *becomes* patient—that is, the behaviors he must engage in in order to earn the title—it becomes apparent that patience is more clearly determined by what a person does *not* do than by what he does. A patient man is one who does not act in a particular way, even though he desires to. He is a man who can endure the temptation to cry out or to complain even though the temptation is strong. Thus patience has to do principally with the control of impulse or its abandonment.

Returning to the situation in our schools, we can see that if students are to face the demands of classroom life with equanimity they must learn to be patient. This means that they must be able to disengage, at least temporarily, their feelings from their actions. It also means, of course, that they must be able to re-engage feelings and actions when conditions are appropriate. In other words, students must wait patiently for their turn to come, but when it does they must still be capable of zestful participation. They must accept the fact of not being called on during a group discussion, but they must continue to volunteer.

Thus, the personal quality commonly described as patience—an essential quality when responding to the demands of the classroom —represents a balance, and sometimes a precarious one, between two opposed tendencies. On the one hand is the impulse to act on desire, to blurt out the answer, to push to the front of the line, or to express anger when interrupted. On the other hand, is the impulse to give up the desire itself, to stop participating in the discussion, to go without a drink when the line is long, or to abandon an interrupted activity.

Whether or not a particular student acquires the desirable balance between impulsive action and apathetic withdrawal depends in part, as has been suggested, on personality qualities that lie outside the scope of the present discussion. In most classrooms powerful social sanctions are in operation to force the student to maintain an attitude of patience. If he impulsively steps out of line his classmates are likely to complain about his being selfish or "pushy." If he shifts over into a state of overt withdrawal, his teacher is apt to call him back to active participation.

But the fact that teachers and peers help to keep a student's behavior in line does not mean that the demands themselves can be ignored. Regardless of his relative success in coping with it, or the forces, personal or otherwise, that might aid in that coping, the elementary school student is situated in a densely populated social world. As curriculum experts and educational technologists try to experiment with new course content and new instructional devices, the crowds in the classroom may be troublesome. But there they are. Part of becoming a student involves learning how to live with that fact.

III

Every child experiences the pain of failure and the joy of success long before he reaches school age, but his achievements, or lack of them, do not really become official until he enters the classroom. From then on, however, a semi-public record of his progress gradually accumulates, and as a student he must learn to adapt to the continued and pervasive spirit of evaluation that will dominate his school years. Evaluation, then, is another important fact of life in the elementary classroom.

As we all know, school is not the only place where a student is made aware of his strengths and weaknesses. His parents make evaluations of him in the home and his friends do likewise in the playground. But the evaluation process that goes on in the classroom is quite different from that which operates in other settings. Accordingly, it presents the student with a set of unique demands to which he must adapt.

The most obvious difference between the way evaluation occurs in school and the way it occurs in other situations is that tests are given in school more frequently than elsewhere. Indeed, with the exception of examinations related to military service or certain kinds of occupations most people seldom encounter tests outside of their school experience.[2] Tests are as indigenous to the school environment as are textbooks or pieces of chalk.

But tests, though they are the classic form of educational evaluation, are not all there is to the process. In fact, in the lower grades

---

[2] There are, of course, the popular quizzes in newspapers and magazines which many people seem to enjoy answering. But these exercises, which might best be called "toy tests," are of little consequence when compared with the real thing that goes on in school.

formal tests are almost nonexistent, although evaluation clearly occurs. Thus the presence of these formal procedures is insufficient to explain the distinctively evaluative atmosphere that pervades the classroom from the earliest grades onward. There is more to it than that.

The dynamics of classroom evaluation are difficult to describe, principally because they are so complex. Evaluations derive from more than one *source,* the *conditions of their communication* may vary in several different ways, they may have one or more of several *referents,* and they may range in *quality* from intensely positive to intensely negative. Moreover, these variations refer only to objective, or impersonal features of evaluation. When the subjective or personal meanings of these events are considered, the picture becomes even more complex. Fortunately, for purposes of the present discussion, we need to focus only on the more objective aspects of the student's evaluative experiences.

The chief *source* of evaluation in the classroom is obviously the teacher. He is called upon continuously to make judgments of students' work and behavior and to communicate that judgment to the students in question and to others. No one who has observed an elementary classroom for any length of time can have failed to be impressed by the vast number of times the teacher performs this function. Typically, in most classrooms students come to know when things are right or wrong, good or bad, pretty or ugly, largely as a result of what the teacher tells them.

But the teacher is not the only one who passes judgment. Classmates frequently join in the act. Sometimes the class as a whole is invited to participate in the evaluation of a student's work, as when the teacher asks, "Who can correct Billy?" or "How many believe that Shirley read that poem with a lot of expression?"[3] At other times the evaluation occurs without any urging from the teacher, as when an egregious error elicits laughter or an outstanding performance wins spontaneous applause.

There is a third source of evaluation in the classroom that is more difficult to describe than are the positive or negative comments coming from teachers and peers. This type of evaluation, which entails self-judgment, occurs without the intervention of an outside judge. When a student is unable to spell any of the words on a spelling test he has been apprized of his failure even if the teacher

---

[3] Jules Henry, an anthropologist, has witnessed signs of what he terms "a witch-hunt syndrome" in several elementary classrooms. A chief component of this syndrome is the destructive criticism of each other by the students, egged on, as it were, by the teacher. See his article, "Attitude organization in elementary school classrooms," *American Journal of Orthopsychiatry,* **27:** 117–133, January 1957.

never sees his paper. When a student works on an arithmetic example at the blackboard he may know that his answer is correct even if the teacher does not bother to tell him so. Thus, as students respond to test questions or complete exercises in their workbooks, or solve problems at the blackboard, they inevitably obtain some information about the quality of their performance. The information is not always correct and may have to be revised by later judgments (Not everyone who thinks he has the right answer really has it!), but, even when wrong, evaluation can leave its mark.

The conditions under which evaluations are communicated add to the complexity of the demands confronting the student. He soon comes to realize, for example, that some of the most important judgments of him and his work are not made known to him at all. Some of these "secret" judgments are communicated to parents; others, such as IQ scores and results of personality tests, are reserved for the scrutiny of school officials only. Judgments made by peers often circulate in the form of gossip or are reported to persons of authority by "tattle-tales." Before he has gone very far in school the student must come to terms with the fact that many things are said about him behind his back.

Those judgments of which the student is aware are communicated with varying degrees of privacy. At one extreme is the public comment made in the presence of other students. In the elementary classroom in particular, students are often praised or admonished in front of their classmates. Perfect papers or "good" drawings are sometimes displayed for all to see. Misbehavior evokes negative sanctions—such as scolding, isolation, removal from the room—that are frequently visible. Before much of the school year has gone by the identity of the "good" students and the "poor" students has become public knowledge in most classrooms.

A less public form of evaluation occurs when the teacher meets privately with the student to discuss his work. Sometimes the student is called to the teacher's desk and sometimes the teacher walks around the room and chats with individuals while the class is engaged in seatwork. Often, however, these seemingly private conferences are secretly attended by eavesdroppers. Thus, it is quite probable, although it might be difficult to prove, that a student's nearest classmates are more intimately aware of the teacher's evaluation of him than are students sitting at a greater distance.

Writing is an even more private means of communicating evaluations than is the spoken word. The terse comment on the margin of a student's paper is the classic form of written evaluation. A variant of this situation occurs when the student answers a self-quiz in his workbook or textbook but does not report his score to anyone. On

21

occasions such as these the student confronts the evaluation of his work in solitude.

Logically, evaluation in the classroom might be expected to be limited chiefly to the student's attainment of educational objectives. And, clearly these limits seem to hold insofar as most of the official evaluations go—the ones that are communicated to parents and entered on school records. But there are at least two other *referents* of evaluation quite common in elementary classrooms. One has to do with the student's adjustment to institutional expectations; the other with his possession of specific character traits. Indeed, the smiles and frowns of teachers and classmates often provide more information about these seemingly peripheral aspects of the student's behavior than they do about his academic progress. Moreover, even when the student's mastery of certain knowledge or skills is allegedly the object of evaluation, other aspects of his behavior commonly are being judged at the same time.

As every school child knows, teachers can become quite angry on occasion. Moreover, every school child quickly learns what makes teachers angry. He learns that in most classrooms the behavior that triggers the teacher's ire has little to do with wrong answers or other indicators of scholastic failure. Rather, it is violations of institutional expectations that really get under the teacher's skin. Typically, when a student is scolded by the teacher it is not because he has failed to spell a word correctly or to grasp the intricacies of long division. He is scolded, more than likely, for coming into the room late, or for making too much noise, or for not listening to directions, or for pushing while in line. Occasionally, teachers do become publicly vexed by their students' academic shortcomings, but to really send them off on a tirade of invective, the young student soon discovers, nothing works better than a partially suppressed giggle during arithmetic period.

The teacher, of course, is not the only source of nonacademic judgments. Evaluation that focuses on a student's personal qualities is as likely to come from his classmates as from anyone else. The student's classroom behavior contributes in large measure to the reputation he develops among his peers for being smart or dumb, a sissy or a bully, teacher's pet or a regular guy, a cheater or a good sport. Most students are fully aware that their behavior is being evaluated in these terms because they judge others in the same way. Classroom friendships and general popularity or unpopularity are based largely on such assessments.[4] Although some of these judg-

[4] Watching these evaluations being made in the classroom (through huddled conferences and the surreptitious exchange of notes) one begins to wonder whether friendship is determined by the possession of special qualities, or whether the qualities are ascribed as a rationalization of friendship or

ments are instantly communicated to the person being evaluated, others are related through intermediaries or friends. Some are so secret that even best friends won't tell.

The teacher's evaluation of the personal qualities of his students typically deals with such matters as general intellectual ability, motivational level, and helpfulness in maintaining a well-run classroom. Such qualities are commonly mentioned on cumulative record folders in terse but telling descriptions. "Johnny has some difficulty with third grade material, but he tries hard," or "Sarah is a neat and pleasant girl. She is a good helper," or, simply, "William is a good worker," are typical of the thumb-nail sketches to be found in abundance in school records. Some teachers, particularly those who pride themselves on being "psychologically sophisticated," also evaluate their students in terms that relate more closely than do the ones already mentioned to the general concept of psychopathology. Aggressiveness and withdrawal are among the traits most frequently mentioned in this connection. Teachers also use the general labels of "problem child" or "disturbed child" for this purpose.

Quite naturally most of the evaluations that have to do with the student's psychological health are not communicated to the student and often not even to the child's parents. Less severe judgments, however, are often made publicly. In the lower grades it is not at all uncommon to hear the teacher, as she gazes over her class, say things like, "I see that John is a good worker," or "Some people (their identities obvious) don't seem to know how to follow directions," or "Liza has a listening face."

The separation of classroom evaluations into those referring to academic attainment, those referring to institutional adjustment, and those referring to possession of personal qualities should not obscure the fact that in many situations all three kinds of assessment are going on at one time. For example, when a student is praised for correctly responding to a teacher's question it may look as though he is simply being rewarded for having the right answer. But obviously there is more to it than that. If the teacher discovered that the student had obtained the answer a few seconds before by reading from a neighbor's paper he would have been punished rather than praised. Similarly, if he had blurted the answer out rather than waiting to be called on he might have received a very different response from the teacher. Thus, it is not just the possession of the right answer but also the way in which it was obtained that

---

enmity that already exists. In many instances it is almost as if the students were saying, "My friends are good guys and my enemies are tattle-tales and cheaters," rather than "Good guys are my friends and tattle-tales and cheaters my enemies." Doubtlessly both kinds of reasoning are in operation in most classrooms.

is being rewarded. In other words, the student is being praised for having achieved and demonstrated intellectual mastery in a prescribed legitimate way. He is being praised, albeit indirectly, for knowing something, for having done what the teacher told him to do, for being a good listener, a cooperative group member, and so on. The teacher's compliment is intended to entice the student (and those who are listening) to engage in certain behaviors in the future, but not simply in the repeated exposure of the knowledge he has just displayed. It is intended to encourage him to do again what the teacher tells him to do, to work hard, to master the material. And so it is with many of the evaluations that appear to relate exclusively to academic matters. Implicitly, they involve the evaluation of many "nonacademic" aspects of the student's behavior.

Evaluations, by definition, connote value. Accordingly, each can be described, at least ideally, according to the kind and degree of value it connotes. Some are positive, others are negative. Some are *very* positive or negative, others are less so. In the classroom, as every one knows, both positive and negative assessments are made and are communicated to students. Teachers scold as well as praise, classmates compliment as well as criticize.

The question of whether smiles are more frequent than frowns, and compliments more abundant than criticisms, depends in part, of course, on the particular classroom under discussion. Some teachers are just not the smiling type, others find it difficult to suppress their grins. The answer also varies dramatically from one student to the next. Some youngsters receive many more negative sanctions than do others, and the same is true with respect to rewards. Conditions also vary for the sexes. From the early grades onward boys are more likely than are girls to violate institutional regulations and, thus, to receive an unequal share of control messages from the teacher. All of these inequalities make it difficult to describe with great accuracy the evaluative setting as it is experienced by any particular child. All that can be said with assurance is that the classroom environment of most students contains some mixture of praise and reproof.

Because both the teacher and his fellow classmates may evaluate a student's behavior, contradictory judgments are possible. A given act may be praised by the teacher and criticized by peers, or vice versa. This may not be the normal state of affairs, to be sure, but it does happen frequently enough to bear comment. A classic example of this kind of a contradiction was observed in one second grade classroom in which a boy was complimented by his teacher for his gracefulness during a period of "creative" dancing while, at the same time, his male classmates teased him for acting like a sissy. This example calls attention to the fact that students are often concerned with the approval of two audiences whose taste may differ. It also hints at the possibility that the conflict between teacher and peer approval might be greater for boys than for girls. Many of the behaviors that the teacher smiles upon, especially those that have to do with compliance to institutional expectations (e.g., neatness, passivity, cleanliness), are more closely linked in our society with feminine than with masculine ideals.

From all that has been said it is evident that learning how to live in a classroom involves not only learning how to handle situations in which one's own work or behavior are evaluated, but also learning how to witness, and occasionally participate in, the evaluation of others. In addition to getting used to a life in which their strengths and weaknesses are often exposed to public scrutiny, students also have to accustom themselves to viewing the strengths and weaknesses of their fellow students. This shared exposure makes comparisons between students inevitable and adds another degree of complexity to the evaluation picture.

The job of coping with evaluation is not left solely to the student. Typically the teacher and other school authorities try to reduce the discomfort that might be associated with some of the harsher aspects of meting out praise and punishment. The dominant viewpoint in education today stresses the pedagogical advantages of success and the disadvantages of failure. In short, our schools are reward-oriented. Thus, teachers are instructed to focus on the good aspects of a student's behavior and to overlook the poor. Indeed, even when a student gives a wrong answer, today's teacher is likely to compliment him for trying. This bias toward the positive does not mean, of course, that negative remarks have disappeared from our schools. But there are certainly fewer of them than there might be if teachers operated under a different set of educational beliefs.

When harsh judgments have to be made, as they often must, teachers often try to conceal them from the class as a whole. Students are called up to the teacher's desk, private conferences are arranged before or after school, test papers are handed back with the grades covered, and so on. Sometimes, when the judgments are very harsh, they are not reported to the student at all. Students are rarely told, for example, that they have been classified as "slow learners" or that the teacher suspects them of having serious emotional problems. Such evaluations, as has been pointed out, are usually the carefully guarded secrets of the school authorities.

School practices covering the communication of positive evaluations are probably less consistent than are those covering negative judgments. Although there is a common tendency to praise students whenever possible, this tendency is usually tempered by the teacher's desire to be fair and "democratic." Thus, the correct answers and perfect papers of students who almost always do good work may be overlooked at times in the interest of giving less able students a chance to bask in the warmth of the teacher's admiration. Most teachers are also sensitive to the fact that lavish praise heaped upon a student may arouse negative evaluations ("teacher's pet," "eager beaver") from his classmates.

Although the student's task in adjusting to evaluation is made easier by common teaching practices, he still has a job to do. In fact, he has three jobs. The first. and most obvious, is to behave in such a way as to enhance the likelihood of praise and reduce the likelihood of punishment. In other words, he must learn how the reward system of the classroom operates and then use that knowledge to increase the flow of rewards to himself. A second job, although one in which students engage with differing degrees of enthusiasm, consists of trying to publicize positive evaluations and conceal negative ones. The pursuit of this goal leads to the practice of carrying good report cards home with pride, and losing poor ones along the way. A third job, and, again, one that may be of greater concern to some students than to others, consists of trying to win the approval of two audiences at the same time. The problem, for some, is how to become a good student while remaining a good guy, how to be at the head of the class while still being in the center of the group.

Most students soon learn that rewards are granted to those who lead a good life. And in school the good life consists, principally, of doing what the teacher says. Of course the teacher says many things, and some of his directions are easier to follow than others, but for the most part his expectations are not seen as unreasonable and the majority of students comply with them sufficiently well to ensure that their hours in the classroom are colored more by praise than by punishment.

But only in very rare instances is compliance the only strategy a student uses to make his way in the evaluative environment of the classroom. Another course of action engaged in by most students at least some of the time is to behave in ways that disguise the failure to comply: in short, to cheat. It may seem unduly severe to label as "cheating" all the little maneuvers that students engage in to cloak aspects of their behavior that might be displeasing to the teacher or their fellow students. Perhaps the term should be reserved to describe the seemingly more serious behavior of trying to falsify performance on a test. But this restriction bestows greater significance than is warranted to test situations and implies that similar behavior in other settings is harmless or hardly worthy of notice.

Yet why should a student who copies an answer from his neighbor's test paper be considered guilty of more serious misbehavior than the student who attempts to misinform by raising his hand when the teacher asks how many have completed their homework assignment? Why is cheating on a test considered a greater breach of educational etiquette than is faking interest during a social studies discussion or sneaking a peek at a comic book during arithmetic class? The answer, presumably, is that performance on tests counts for more, in that it is preserved as a lasting mark on the student's record. And that answer might justify the differences in our attitudes toward these various practices. But it should not permit us to overlook the fact that copying an answer on a test, feigning interest during a discussion, giving a false answer to a teacher's query, and disguising forbidden activities are all of a piece. Each represents an effort to avoid censure or to win unwarranted praise. Such efforts are far more common in the classroom than our focus on cheating in test situations would have us believe. Learning how to make it in school involves, in part, learning how to falsify our behavior.

There is another way of coping with evaluations that warrants mention even though it is not deserving of the term "strategy." This method entails devaluing the evaluations to a point where they no longer matter very much. The student who has adopted this alternative over those of complying or cheating has learned how to "play it cool" in the classroom. He is neither elated by success nor deflated by failure. He may indeed try to "stay out of trouble" in the classroom and thus comply with the teacher's minimal expectations, but this is principally because getting into trouble entails further entanglements and involvement with school officials and other adults, a situation that he would prefer to avoid.

This brief description of emotional detachment from school affairs has two shortcomings. It makes the process sound more rational than it probably is and it focuses on a rather extreme form of the condition. Students do not likely *decide* to become uninvolved with school in the same way that they decide to collect baseball cards or to visit a sick friend. Rather, their lack of involvement likely has a causal history of which they are only dimly aware at best. The way in which such an attitude might slowly develop without the student being acutely conscious of it is one of the major topics to be discussed in the next chapter. Also, detachment is surely not an either/or state of affairs. Students cannot be sharply divided into the involved and the uninvolved. Rather, all students probably learn to employ psychological buffers that protect them from some of the wear and tear of classroom life. To anyone who has been in a classroom it is also evident that some students end up being more insulated than others.

Before leaving the topic of evaluation in the classroom, attention must be given to a distinction that has enjoyed wide currency in educational discussions. This is the distinction between "extrinsic" motivation (doing school work for the rewards it will bring in the form of good grades and teacher approval) on the one hand, and "intrinsic" motivation (doing school work for the pleasure that comes from the task itself) on the other. If we want children to continue to learn after they leave the classroom, so the argument goes, it would be wise gradually to de-emphasize the importance of grades and other "extrinsic" rewards and concentrate instead on having the student derive his major satisfactions from the learning activities themselves. An illustration often used in making this point involves the child's progress in learning how to play the piano. When piano lessons are first begun the student may have to be forced to practice through the use of external rewards and punishments. But after a time, hopefully, the student will derive such pleasure from the skill itself that rewards and punishments will no longer be very important.

The trouble with the piano-playing illustration and with the whole concept of intrinsic and extrinsic motivation as it relates to classroom activity is that it does not take into account the complexity of the evaluations that occur there. If classroom rewards and punishments only had to do with whether the students practiced their spelling or their arithmetic, life for both the teacher and his students would be much simpler. But, clearly, reality is more complicated than that.

The notion of intrinsic motivation begins to lose some of its power when applied to behaviors other than those that involve academic knowledge or skills. What about behaviors that deal with conformity to institutional expectations? What kind of intrinsic motivation can the teacher appeal to when he wants students to be silent even though they want to talk? It is true that he might make a logical appeal to them rather than merely telling them to shut up, but it is hard to imagine that the students will ever find anything intrinsically satisfying about being silent when they wish to talk. And the same thing is true for many aspects of classroom behavior that arouse evaluative comments from teachers and students. Thus, the goal of making classroom activities intrinsically satisfying to students turns out to be unattainable except with respect to a narrowly circumscribed set of behavior.

IV

The fact of unequal power is a third feature of classroom life to which students must become accustomed. The difference in authority between the teacher and his students is related, quite obviously, to the evaluative aspects of classroom life. But it involves much more than the distribution of praise and reproof. This difference provides the most salient feature of the social structure of the classroom and its consequences relate to the broader conditions of freedom, privilege, and responsibility as manifest in classroom affairs.

One of the earliest lessons a child must learn is how to comply with the wishes of others. Soon after he becomes aware of the world he is in, the newborn infant becomes conscious of one of the main features of that world: adult authority. As he moves from home to school the authority of parents is gradually supplemented by control from teachers, the second most important set of adults in his life. But early parental authority differs in several important ways from that which he will confront in school and these differences are important for understanding the character of the classroom environment.

Two of the chief differences between the parent's relationship with his child and the teacher's with his student have to do with the intimacy and duration of the contact. The emotional ties between parents and children are usually stronger and last longer than those between teachers and students. This does not mean, of course, that students never feel close to their teachers, and vice versa. We know that a child's relationship with his teacher can at times rival in intensity the union between him and his mother and father. We also know that teachers are occasionally attracted toward particular students in an intense and personal way. But still the dominant relationship in the classroom is quite impersonal when compared with that which goes on in the home.

The reduced intimacy in the classroom as compared with the home has to do not only with the intensity of feelings among participants but also with the extent to which the participants have been exposed to each other in a variety of poses and guises. Members of a household come to know each other physically as well as psychologically, in a way that almost never happens in the classroom. Also, family members share a personal history in a way that members of other groups do not. Consequently, parents and children are likely to have a much more extensive familiarity with each other than are teachers and students.

The relative impersonality and narrowness of the teacher-student relationship has consequences for the way in which authority is handled in the classroom. It is there that students must learn to take orders from adults who do not know them very well and whom they do not themselves know intimately. For the first time in the child's life, power that has personal consequences for the child himself is wielded by a relative stranger.

Perhaps one of the chief differences between the authority of parents and teachers, although not the most obvious, has to do with the purposes for which their power is put to use. Parents, by and large, are principally restrictive. Their chief concern, at least during the child's early years, is with prohibiting action, with telling the child what *not* to do. Parental authority during the pre-school years is characterized by the commands, "Stop!" and "Don't!" It is an authority whose chief goal is to place limits on natural impulses and spontaneous interests, particularly when those impulses and interests endanger the child himself or threaten to destroy something of value to the parent. The infant's playpen symbolizes the type of authority with which children must learn to live during their early years. This ubiquitous piece of child-rearing equipment places definite limits on the child's sphere of activity, but within that sphere he is free to do almost anything he wishes.

The teacher's authority, in contrast, is as much prescriptive as restrictive. Teachers are concerned with setting assignments for students rather than with merely curbing undesirable behavior. Their authority is characterized as much by "Do" as by "Don't." Just as the playpen is symbolic of the parent's commands so is the desk symbolic of the commands issued by teachers. The desk represents not just a limited sphere of activity but a setting specially designed for a very narrow range of behavior. Seated at his desk the student is in the position to do something. It is the teacher's job to declare what that something shall be.

At the heart of the teacher's authority is his command over the student's attention. Students are expected to attend to certain matters while they are in the classroom, and much of the teacher's energies are spent in making sure that this happens. At home the child must learn how to stop; at school he must learn how to look and listen.

Another view of the teacher's authority might focus on the process of substitution by which the teacher's plans for action are substituted for the student's own. When students do what the teacher tells them to do they are, in effect, abandoning one set of plans (their own) in favor of another (their teacher's). At times, of course, these two sets of plans do not conflict and may even be quite similar. But at other times that which is given up in no way resembles the action called for by the teacher. The lack of resemblance between the teacher's plans and the student's own must partially account for the difficulty some students have in adjusting to the classroom, but the relationship between these two states of affairs is surely not simple. The important point is that students must learn to employ their executive powers in the service of the teacher's desires rather than their own. Even if it hurts.

The distinction between work and play has far-reaching consequences for human affairs, and the classroom is the setting in which most people encounter this distinction in a personally meaningful way. According to one of its many definitions, work entails becoming engaged in a purposeful activity that has been prescribed for us by someone else; an activity in which we would not at that moment be engaged if it were not for some system of authority relationships. As pre-schoolers the students may have played with the concept of work, but their fanciful enactments of adult work situations usually lack one essential ingredient, namely: the use of some kind of an external authority system to tell them what to do and to keep them at their job. The teacher, with his prescriptive dicta and his surveillance over the students' attention, provides the missing ingredient that makes work real. The teacher, although he may disclaim the title, is the student's first "Boss."

The worker, almost by definition, is a person who is tempted, from time to time, to abandon his role. Presumably there are other things he would rather be doing, but his boss's eye, or his need for money, or the voice of his inner conscience keep him at the job. Sometimes, of course, he yields to his temptation, either by taking the day off or, when conditions become intolerable, by quitting his job. The right to leave the work situation varies greatly from one job to another, but the ultimate privilege, that of quitting, is open to all adults. Any worker, if he doesn't like his job, can throw down his tools and walk away. He may live to regret his decision, but the decision to leave is his.

But consider the plight of the young student. If a third grader should refuse to obey the system of bells that tell him when to enter and when to leave the classroom, the wheels of retributive justice would begin to grind. And the teacher would sound the alarm that would put them in motion. This fact calls attention to an important aspect of the teacher's use of authority. As has been pointed out, schools resemble so-called total institutions, such as prisons, mental hospitals, and the like, in that one subgroup of their clientele (the students) are involuntarily committed to the institution, whereas another subgroup (the staff) has greater freedom of movement and, most important, has the ultimate freedom to leave the institution entirely. Under these circumstances it is common for the more privileged group to guard the exits, either figuratively or literally. Again, teachers may not like this description and may, in protesting, insist that they operate "democratic" classrooms, but in a very real sense their responsibilities bear some resemblance to those of prison guards. In "progressive" prisons, as in most classrooms, the inhabitants are allowed certain freedoms, but there are real limits. In both institutions the inmates might be allowed to plan a Christmas party, but in neither place are they allowed to plan a "break."

The starkness of the difference in power between teachers and students may be heightened or subdued depending on school policy and the personal predilections of the teachers. Many of the differences between so-called traditional and progressive institutions derive from the ways in which the teacher's authority is handled. In some schools, for example, students are required to rise when the teacher enters the room, whereas in others they are encouraged to call the teacher by his first name. In some schools students have little or no say in determining the content of the curriculum, whereas in others pupil-planning is used as a procedure for increasing the "meaningfulness" of the students' experience. But, even in the most progressive environments, the teacher is very much in control and pupils usually are aware of the centrality and power of his position. Even a first grader knows that an absent teacher requires a substitute, whereas an absent student does not.

In the best of all possible worlds it is expected that children will adapt to the teacher's authority by becoming "good workers" and "model students." And, by and large, this ideal comes close to being realized. Most students learn to look and to listen when told to and to keep their private fantasies in check when class is in session. Moreover, this skill in complying with educational authority is doubly important because the student will be called upon to put it to work in many out-of-school settings. The transition from classroom to factory or office is made easily by those who have developed "good work habits" in their early years.

But not all students become good workers, and even those who do are sometimes forced to employ "shady" practices when dealing with the teacher's authority. Under conditions of grossly unequal power such as exists in classrooms, two types of interpersonal maneuvering almost inevitably arise. The first involves the seeking of special favor. One way of managing life in a total institution is by moving close to the sources of power during the off-hours and behaving in ways that cause authorities to respond favorably. At the more manipulative and cynical extreme this strategy involves fawning, false compliments, and other forms of social dishonesty. These extreme practices which might be referred to collectively as "apple polishing" are usually accompanied by feelings of cynicism or self-hatred. Less extreme variations include merely "being helpful" and "creating a good impression." In adult society this strategy leads to the practice of bringing the boss home for dinner. The classroom equivalent of dinner for the boss is the traditional apple for the teacher.

A second tactic that is in some ways the reverse of the first involves the practice of hiding words and deeds that might displease the authorities. It takes effort to create a good impression but it also requires work to avoid creating a bad one. Just as some of the pupil's energies are spent in trying to please the teacher, so are others spent in trying to keep out of trouble. The secrecy that frequently develops in total institutions is aligned, at least in part, with the authority structure. Certainly this is true in school. Teachers keep secrets from their principals as do students from their teachers. But not all of these secrets have to do with the avoidance of a negative evaluation from authority figures. Some may have as their goal the manipulation of institutional privileges. When, for example, a teacher asks a student if he has already been to the drinking fountain that morning and he untruthfully says "no," it is not because a truthful answer would provoke the teacher but because it might destroy the chances of his getting a second drink. So it is with many of the minor subterfuges that are commonplace in the classroom.

Because the oppressive use of power is antithetical to our democratic ideals it is difficult to discuss its normal occurrence in the classroom without arousing concern. The concepts of obedience and of independence are often thought to be antithetical and, in our society, the latter concept is more often the declared objective of our schools than is the former. Therefore, we typically play down or fail to recognize the extent to which students are expected to conform to the expectations of others and when this state of affairs is called to our attention the natural response is one of alarm.

Yet the habits of obedience and docility engendered in the classroom have a high pay-off value in other settings. So far as their power structure is concerned classrooms are not too dissimilar from factories or offices, those ubiquitous organizations in which so much of our adult life is spent. Thus, school might really be called a preparation for life, but not in the usual sense in which educators employ that slogan. Power may be abused in school as elsewhere, but its existence is a fact of life to which we must adapt. The process of adaptation begins during the first few years of life but it is significantly accelerated, for most of us, on the day we enter kindergarten.

V

As implied in the title of this chapter, the crowds, the praise, and the power that combine to give a distinctive flavor to classroom life collectively form a hidden curriculum which each student (and teacher) must master if he is to make his way satisfactorily through the school. The demands created by these features of classroom life may be contrasted with the academic demands—the "official" curriculum, so to speak—to which educators traditionally have paid the most attention. As might be expected, the two curriculums are related to each other in several important ways.

As has already been suggested in the discussion of praise in the classroom, the reward system of the school is linked to success in both curriculums. Indeed, many of the rewards and punishments that sound as if they are being dispensed on the basis of academic success and failure are really more closely related to the mastery of the hidden curriculum. Consider, as an instance, the common teaching practice of giving a student credit for trying. What do teachers mean when they say a student tries to do his work? They mean, in essence, that he complies with the procedural expectations of the institution. He does his homework (though incorrectly), he raises his hand during class discussion (though he usually comes up with the wrong answer), he keeps his nose in his book during free study period (though he doesn't turn the page very often). He is, in other words, a "model" student, though not necessarily a good one.

It is difficult to imagine any of today's teachers, particularly those in elementary schools, failing a student who tries, even though his mastery of course content is slight. Indeed, even at higher levels of education rewards sometimes go to the meek as well as the mighty. It is certainly possible that many of our valedictorians and presidents of our honor societies owe their success as much to institutional conformity as to intellectual prowess. Although it offends our sensibilities to admit it, no doubt that bright-eyed little girl who stands trembling before the principal on graduation day arrived there at least in part because she typed her weekly themes neatly and handed her homework in on time.

This manner of talking about educational affairs may sound cynical and may be interpreted as a criticism of teachers or as an attempt to subvert the virtues of neatness, punctuality, and courteous conduct in general. But nothing of that kind is intended. The point is simply that in schools, as in prisons, good behavior pays off.

Just as conformity to institutional expectations can lead to praise, so can the lack of it lead to trouble. As a matter of fact, the relationship of the hidden curriculum to student difficulties is even more striking than is its relationship to student success. As an instance, consider the conditions leading to disciplinary action in the classroom. Why do teachers scold students? Because the student has given a wrong answer? Because, try as he might, he fails to grasp the intricacies of long division? Not usually. Rather, students are commonly scolded for coming into the room late or for making too much noise or for not listening to the teacher's directions or for pushing while in line. The teacher's wrath, in other words, is more frequently triggered by violations of institutional regulations and routines than by signs of his students' intellectual deficiencies.

Even when we consider the more serious difficulties that clearly entail academic failure, the demands of the hidden curriculum lurk in the background. When Johnny's parents are called in to school because their son is not doing too well in arithmetic, what explanation is given for their son's poor performance? Typically, blame is placed on motivational deficiencies in Johnny rather than on his intellectual shortcomings. The teacher may even go so far as to say that Johnny is *un*motivated during arithmetic period. But what does this mean? It means, in essence, that Johnny does not even try. And not trying, as we have seen, usually boils down to a failure to comply with institutional expectations, a failure to master the hidden curriculum.

Testmakers describe a person as "test-wise" when he has caught on to the tricks of test construction sufficiently well to answer questions correctly even though he does not know the material on which he is being examined. In the same way one might think of students as becoming "school-wise" or "teacher-wise" when they have discovered how to respond with a minimum amount of pain and discomfort to the demands, both official and unofficial of classroom life. Schools, like test items, have rules and traditions of their own that can only be mastered through successive exposure. But with schools as with tests all students are not equally adroit. All are asked to respond but not everyone catches on to the rules of the game.

If it is useful to think of there being two curriculums in the classroom, a natural question to ask about the relationship between them is whether their joint mastery calls for compatible or contradictory personal qualities. That is, do the same strengths that contribute to intellectual achievement also contribute to the student's success in conformity to institutional expectations? This question likely has no definite answer, but it is thought-provoking and even a brief consideration of it leads into a thicket of educational and psychological issues.

It is probably safe to predict that general ability, or intelligence, would be an asset in meeting all of the demands of school life, whether academic or institutional. The child's ability to understand causal relationships, as an instance, would seem to be of as much service as he tries to come to grips with the rules and regulations of classroom life as when he grapples with the rudiments of plant chemistry. His verbal fluency can be put to use as easily in "snowing" the teacher as in writing a short story. Thus, to the extent that the demands of classroom life call for rational thought, the student with superior intellectual ability would seem to be at an advantage.

But more than ability is involved in adapting to complex situations. Much also depends upon attitudes, values, and life style—upon all those qualities commonly grouped under the term: *personality*. When the contribution of personality to adaptive strategy is considered, the old adage of "the more, the better," which works so well for general ability, does not suffice. Personal qualities that are beneficial in one setting may be detrimental in another. Indeed, even a single setting may make demands that call upon competing or conflicting tendencies in a person's makeup.

We have already seen that many features of classroom life call for patience, at best, and resignation, at worst. As he learns to live in school our student learns to subjugate his own desires to the will of the teacher and to subdue his own actions in the interest of the common good. He learns to be passive and to acquiesce to the network of rules, regulations, and routines in which he is embedded. He learns to tolerate petty frustrations and accept the plans and policies of higher authorities, even when their rationale is unexplained and their meaning unclear. Like the inhabitants of most other institutions, he learns how to shrug and say, "That's the way the ball bounces."

But the personal qualities that play a role in intellectual mastery are very different from those that characterize the Company Man. Curiosity, as an instance, that most fundamental of all scholarly traits, is of little value in responding to the demands of conformity. The curious person typically engages in a kind of probing, poking, and exploring that is almost antithetical to the attitude of the passive conformist. The scholar must develop the habit of challenging authority and of questioning the value of tradition. He must insist on explanations for things that are unclear. Scholarship requires discipline, to be sure, but this discipline serves the demands of scholarship rather than the wishes and desires of other people. In short, intellectual mastery calls for sublimated forms of aggression rather than for submission to constraints.

This brief discussion likely exaggerates the real differences between the demands of institutional conformity and the demands of scholarship, but it does serve to call attention to points of possible conflict. How incompatible are these two sets of demands? Can both be mastered by the same person? Apparently so. Certainly not all of our student council presidents and valedictorians can be dismissed as weak-willed teacher's pets, as academic Uriah Heeps. Many students clearly manage to maintain their intellectual aggressiveness while at the same time acquiescing to the laws that govern the social traffic of our schools. Apparently it *is* possible, under certain conditions, to breed "docile scholars," even though the expression seems to be a contradiction in terms. Indeed, certain forms of scholarship have been known to flourish in monastic settings, where the demands for institutional conformity are extreme.

Unfortunately, no one seems to know how these balances are maintained, nor even how to establish them in the first place. But even more unfortunate is the fact that few if any school people are giving the matter serious thought. As institutional settings multiply and become for more and more people the areas in which a significant portion of their life is enacted, we will need to know much more than we do at present about how to achieve a reasonable synthesis between the forces that drive a person to seek individual expression and those that drive him to comply with the wishes of others. Presumably what goes on in classrooms contributes significantly to this synthesis. The school is the first major institution, outside the family, in which almost all of us are immersed. From kindergarten onward, the student begins to learn what life is really like in The Company.

The demands of classroom life discussed in this chapter pose problems for students and teachers alike. As we have seen, there are many methods for coping with these demands and for solving the problems they create. Moreover, each major adaptive strategy is subtly transformed and given a unique expression as a result of the idiosyncratic characteristics of the student employing it. Thus, the total picture of adjustment to school becomes infinitely complex as it is manifested in the behavior of individual students.

Yet certain commonalities do exist beneath all the complexity created by the uniqueness of individuals. No matter what the demand or the personal resources of the person facing it there is at least one strategy open to all. This is the strategy of psychological withdrawal, of gradually reducing personal concern and involvement to a point where neither the demand nor one's success or failure in coping with it is sharply felt. Chapter 3 focuses exclusively on this all-purpose strategy, detachment, as it is employed in the classroom. In order to better understand student tactics, however, it is important to consider the climate of opinion from which they emerge. Before focusing on what they do in the classroom, we must examine how students feel about school.

Students' Feelings about School 2

The real question is whether it is still normal for a school child to live for years amid irrational terrors and lunatic misunderstandings. And here one is really up against the very great difficulty of knowing what a child really feels and thinks. A child which appears reasonably happy may actually be suffering horrors which it cannot or will not reveal.

George Orwell, "Such were the days," in
A Collection of Essays by George Orwell

The emphasis in Chapter 1 on the repetitive, routinized, and compulsory aspects of classroom life may give the impression that school is an unpleasant place to be. And certainly it must be for some students, some of the time. Yet, as has also been noted, we know that the classroom is seen as a delightful and exciting place to be by others. How diverse are students' feelings about their academic life? Which feelings predominate, the positive or the negative? Furthermore, what is the educational significance of the attitudes that do exist? Can teachers tell which are the contented students and which are the unhappy ones? And even if they could make such a distinction, ought they to bother doing so? Are attitudes toward school significantly related to the quality of educational performance?

Although questions such as these sound direct enough, they lack simple answers. Moreover, despite their apparent directness and importance, not all of these questions have undergone serious scrutiny by educators and research workers. Consequently, as we seek answers to them we must be content with scraps of evidence instead of definitive findings. We must also be prepared to consider subjective testimony as well as objective fact.

I

Both the pleasures and the pains of school life, and particularly of life in the earlier grades, have been celebrated in song and story. A pleasant nostalgia steals over some of us as we hum the lines: "School days, school days, dear old Golden Rule days." But Shakespeare, with characteristic candor, reminds us that not all the days were that sunny for "the whining school boy, with his satchel and shining morning face, creeping like snail unwillingly to school." And if we were to continue our literary search the evidence would accumulate on both sides of the issue. In other words, adults who have bothered to describe their childhood experiences make it clear that the classroom was heaven for some, hell for others, and a bit of both for most.

Among negative reports of school life two themes predominate. The first has to do with frightening or embarrassing experiences resulting from the actions of cruel or insensitive teachers and classmates. Stories of unusually severe punishments and of being the object of ridicule characterize such reports. The second theme has to do with feelings of boredom arising from the meaninglessness of the assigned tasks or the overwhelming attractiveness of life outside the class. In descriptions of the first type the narrator's pain is often reported to have been public and acute. In descriptions of the second type the narrator typically portrays himself as having suffered in silence.

Accounts of unusual punishment, particularly physical punishment, at the hands of teachers are not as plentiful today as they likely were a generation or so ago. There are two major reasons for this change. First, many of our states have established legal restrictions to the teacher's use of corporal punishment. The public school teacher of today who is tempted to strike a child runs the risk, if he acts on his impulse, of getting involved in a law suit or of losing his job. Second, and more important, the practice of physical punishment is antithetical to the educational ideas that guide today's teaching practice. Modern teachers are advised to be understanding, to "meet the needs" of their charges, to be warm and "supporting." Many, if not most, teachers try to follow such advice and to avoid being harshly punitive.

For a description of a type of classroom discomfort that is rare nowadays we must turn to the recollection of older adults, or ones who were educated in other cultures. George Orwell, as an instance, related a kind of Dickensian school experience which, while seemingly extreme, is probably not too far removed from the experience of many adults who received their elementary schooling in this country a generation or two ago or who, at a more recent date, went to a private or foreign school that eschewed a more "enlightened" philosophy. Here is school as Orwell remembered it.

> We would sit round the long shiny table, made of some very pale-coloured, hard wood, with Sim (the teacher) goading, threatening, exhorting, sometimes joking, very occasionally praising, but always prodding, prodding away at one's mind to keep it up to the right pitch of concentration, as one might keep a sleepy person awake by sticking pins into him.

> "Go on, you little slacker! Go on, you idle, worthless little boy! The whole trouble with you is that you're bone and horn idle. You eat too much, that's why. You wolf down enormous meals, and then when you come here you're half

asleep. Go on, now, put your back into it. You're not *thinking*. Your brain doesn't sweat."

He would tap away at one's skull with his silver pencil, which, in my memory, seems to have been about the size of a banana, and which certainly was heavy enough to raise a bump: or he would pull the short hairs round one's ears, or, occasionally, reach out under the table and kick one's shin. On some days nothing seemed to go right, and then it would be: "All right, then, I know what you want. You've been asking for it the whole morning. Come along, you useless little slacker. Come into the study." And then whack, whack, whack, whack, and back one would come, red-wealed and smarting—in later years Sim had abandoned his riding crop in favor of a thin rattan cane which hurt very much more—to settle down to work again.[1]

Other examples might be given but Orwell's account is probably sufficient to remind us that the school day memories of many adults have been seared by encounters with cruel and despotic teachers. No one knows just how frequent such experiences are, but certainly they are not common in today's schools. Of course, the fact that teachers rarely spank their students does not mean that cruelty has disappeared from the classroom. The hickory stick was not the only weapon at the teacher's disposal, and from a psychological point of view, surely not the most painful one. Nonetheless, cruelty, in its many guises, is probably not central in the memories carried from today's classrooms, even though it may continue to be of overwhelming significance for a small number of students.

A second, and perhaps more common, memory of classroom discomfort is one in which feelings of tedium dominate. A recollection colored by such feeling is provided by George Santayana in the following description of life in Boston's Boys' Latin School:

Each room had four great windows, but the street and the courts at the side and rear were narrow, and over-shadowed by houses or office-buildings. No blackboard was black; all were indelibly clouded with ingrained layers of old chalk; the more you rubbed it out, the more you rubbed it in. Every desk was stained with generations of ink-spots, cut deeply with initials and scratched drawings. What idle thoughts had been wandering for years through all those empty heads in all those tedious school hours! In the best schools, almost

[1] George Orwell, "Such were the days" in *A Collection of Essays by George Orwell* (New York: Doubleday, 1954), pp. 17–18.

all schooltime is wasted. Now and then something is learned that sticks fast; for the rest the boys are merely given time to grow and are kept from too much mischief.[2]

A more recent image of boredom in the classroom, and one that likely is more evocative for today's readers, is contained in the following description by an author who is recalling life in America in the mid-Thirties.

> Imagine yourself thirteen summers young in a world that stretched as far as the eye could see, but no further; a world of boring visits to ancient aunts and Sunday drives and triple features, plus serial and two cartoons, of baseball in the streets and zoos and jawbreakers and Indian gum and penmanship and firecrackers and Tarzan and the Scarecrow. It's morning. Off to the grey prison, school, and the heavy books, the ceramic women with their fiery eyes, and the clock-hands that never moved. One o'clock. A century later, two o'clock. Two centuries later, three o'clock. Saved by the bell![3]

Other examples of the theme of boredom surely could be added, but the two that have been given should suffice to make the point: for many people life in school, at least as preserved in adult memories of that life, is often portrayed as having been dull and wearisome. As was true for reports of teachers' cruelty, it is difficult to judge from these written accounts how pervasive such feelings might be in a typical classroom, but they obviously occur frequently enough to be understood and sympathized with by the narrator's audience. Moreover, some of the features of classroom life to be discussed in later chapters, lead us to suspect that the dull ache of boredom may be more common in our schools than occasional literary accounts would lead us to suspect.

In order to balance the picture of school day memories some attention must be given to the other extreme, to happy recollections of classroom life. For though school was painful and dull for some, it was pleasurable and exciting for others. In fact, the heights of elation and the depths of despair connected with school events are often contained within the childhood memory of one person. The child who trudged to school on one day often raced there on the next. Even Orwell, in the midst of his gloomy account of life at Crossgates, is forced to admit, "No one can look back on his school days and say with truth that they were altogether unhappy."[4]

---

[2] George Santayana, *Persons and Places* (New York: Scribner, 1944), p. 154.
[3] Charles Beaumont, *Remember? Remember?* (New York: Macmillan, 1963), p. 49.
[4] Orwell, p. 25.

As Orwell's experience reminds us, teachers can sometimes be very cruel or otherwise behave stupidly, but they may exhibit positive virtues as well as negative ones. Fortunately, the memories of some students are crowded with the pleasures of these early encounters. Thomas Wolfe, in a letter praising his childhood teacher, Mrs. Roberts, provides a memorable example of how some adults feel about certain aspects of their school experience.

> During the years Mrs. Roberts taught me she exercised an influence that is inestimable on almost every particular of my life and thought.
> With the other boys of my age I know she did the same. We turned instinctively to this lady for her advice and direction and we trusted to it unfalteringly.
> I think that kind of relation is one of the profoundest experiences of anyone's life,—I put the relation of a fine teacher to a student just below the relation of a mother to her son and I don't think I could say more than this.[5]

Considering the number of teachers a child encounters as he passes through school, it is unlikely that all, or even many, of them will be recalled with the degree of fondness contained in Wolfe's letter. Indeed, we might wonder how many students ever have such a memorable educational experience. But the teacher's personal influence need not be particularly profound in order for the student to retain fond memories of his days in the classroom. Consider, for example, the following account in which the names of specific teachers never appear.

> My neophyte awe had not abated: the moment Mademoiselle entered the classroom, every second became holy. Our teachers didn't tell us anything wildly exciting; we would recite our lessons, and they would correct our homework; but I asked for nothing more than that my existence should be publicly sanctioned by them. . . . These glittering moments shone like beacons down the year: each day was leading me further on. I felt sorry for grown-ups whose uneventful weeks are only feebly brightened by the dullness of Sundays.[6]

Here, then, are a handful of descriptions of extreme feelings connected with schools and schooling. Each makes interesting reading and together they provide striking evidence of the lasting

---

[5] Thomas Wolfe, "A letter of gratitude and indebtedness," in Claude M. Fuess and Emory S. Basford (eds.), *Unseen Harvests* (New York: Macmillan, 1947), p. 438.
[6] Simone deBeauvoir, *Memoirs of a Dutiful Daughter* (New York: Random House, 1963), pp. 66–67.

impact that school events may have on our lives. But how much do these descriptions teach us about the experience of spending thousands of hours in classrooms? Unfortunately, the answer would seem to be: relatively little. There are several reasons why this is so.

Although particular school experiences clearly have been occasions of joy for some people and of hatred for others, all varieties of emotion between the extremes of joy and hatred doubtlessly have been felt by some students some of the time. But mild emotions are not too interesting to hear about and, therefore, they likely are not described as often as are those that hold the reader's attention. As another source of bias, autobiographical accounts tend to be written chiefly by people of note. Thus, from such accounts we may be able to learn something about what school meant to a small number of authors or famous scientists or statesmen, but the recollections of housewives or accountants or salesmen rarely get into print. In other words, we can learn a little about what school must have been like for a very select group of highly articulate people but it is unsafe to trust the representativeness of these reports. Moreover, in the last analysis we have no guarantee that school days recollected in the tranquility of adulthood provide a trustworthy picture of the immediate experience of living in a classroom. Memory, as we know, has a way of becoming distorted with time. Those long afternoons in the third grade may not look so bad from a distance of twenty or thirty years. Conversely, the delight that filled many of our childhood hours may be eclipsed by the more immediate pleasures of our adult life.

For these reasons, among others, it is wise to avoid relying too heavily on adult memories as a source of insight into the students' world. However much we might enjoy reading such accounts we had better move up closer to the immediate experience of young children if we are to discover what life in the classroom is really like. In short, we had better get to our informants while the smudge of chalk dust is still on their sleeves.

Strangely enough not too much is known about how young children themselves look upon their school experience. This fact is particularly surprising in a day when it has become almost a national pastime to find out how people feel about things. We do seem to become mildly interested in learning about student opinion by the time the students have reached high school, and on our college campuses the pollsters are almost as plentiful as in the supermarket. But grade school student's sentiment with regard to classroom life is relatively unexplored.

Among the few studies that have been conducted one of the most interesting was undertaken about 25 years ago by Samuel

Tenenbaum, who was then a New York City high school teacher.[7] Tenenbaum constructed a questionnaire consisting of 20 straight-forward statements about the respondent's attitudes toward his school, his teacher, and his classmates. The following is a typical item:

I am happy in school
    a. all the time.
    b. most of the time.
    c. pretty often.
    d. hardly ever.
    e. never.

This questionnaire, which appears to have been constructed with reasonable care,[8] was administered to 639 sixth and seventh grade students enrolled in three New York City schools situated in high, middle, and low income areas of the city. Each student also wrote a brief essay in response to the question: "Do you like school?" All answers were submitted anonymously and no teachers or supervisors were present during the testing sessions.

Responses to the essay questionnaire provide the clearest summary of Tenenbaum's findings. Each essay was judged to reflect one of three attitudes toward school—liking, disliking, or having mixed feelings—with the following results.

Table 1   *Student Responses to the Question:*
"Do You Like School?"[a]

	BOYS	GIRLS	TOTAL
Like school	48.6%	69.0%	58.8%
Dislike school	23.8%	10.3%	17.1%
Have mixed feelings	27.6%	20.7%	24.1%

[a] From Tenenbaum, "Uncontrolled expressions of children's attitudes toward school," *Elementary School Journal,* **40**: 670–678, May 1940.

---

[7] Tenenbaum's work is reported in four separate articles. These are: "A test to measure a child's attitude toward school, teachers, and classmates," *Educational Administration and Supervision* 26:176–188, March 1940; "Uncontrolled expressions of children's attitudes toward school," *Elementary School Journal,* **40**:670–678, May 1940; "A school attitude questionnaire test correlated with such variables as IQ, EQ, past and present grade marks, absence and grade progress," *Educational Administration and Supervision,* 27:107–124, February 1941; and "Attitudes of elementary school children to school, teachers, and classmates," *Journal of Applied Psychology,* 28:134–141, April 1944.

[8] Tenenbaum reports a reliability coefficient (internal consistency) of .85 for the instrument as a whole and .91 for the fourteen items dealing with general school attitudes. He also describes as successful his efforts to assess

Two aspects of this summary require special comment. First, even though the majority of the responses were judged to contain expressions of positive feelings, the percentage of negative sentiments is too large to be ignored. Although a quick reading of these results would lead to the conclusion that most students like school, it is equally valid to conclude that somewhere between one-third and one-half of the students have their doubts about the matter. Second, girls have more positive feelings toward school than do boys. Slightly less than half the boys had clearly positive feelings as compared with a little more than two-thirds of the girls. This sex difference, which confirms what most people probably would have predicted, appears in several studies and will be the subject of further comment in this and subsequent chapters.

Tenenbaum's comments on the content of the essays provide further information useful in interpreting the summary statistics. He remarks on the relative absence of strong sentiment in the students' responses. In his judgment, many responses tended to be stereotyped and to follow "conventional patterns." He also notes that the responses often had an "adult character" about them. These qualities of the students' writings lead him to conclude,

> The study reveals the seriousness of children excepting [sic] in infrequent instances. They do not look at school as a place of joy or pleasure. There is no exuberant enthusiasm displayed. There is no zestful approach to the school situation The children attend school with consciousness that it will help them out in later life. School is not pleasurable for itself. It is important for its future promise.[9]

The feelings expressed in the student's essays are broadly corroborated by their responses to the questionnaire itself. The amount of open discontent expressed on each of the questions dealing with school life in general seems to hover around 20 percent. For example, 21 percent of the students claim to be "sad at the thought of going to school"; 22.2 percent indicate that they "do not like school" (as compared with 17.1 percent in the "Dislike" category on the essay); 23 percent say they "would rather work than go to school." Interestingly enough this margin of discontent is noticeably reduced when the questions focus on the teachers or fellow students rather than school in general. Only 8 percent of the

---

the concurrent validity of the questionnaire by comparing it with results obtained through personal interview. In preparation for developing subscores on the questionnaire, independent judges decided whether each question dealt principally with school in general, teachers, or classmates. Agreement among the judges was almost perfect.

[9] Tenenbaum, "Uncontrolled expressions of children's attitudes toward school," p. 675.

students express a dislike for their present teachers and just 6 percent indicate a dislike for teachers as a group. Roughly, the same percentages are obtained in response to questions dealing with schoolmates. In other words, it seems as if it were the institution of the school rather than the specific people it houses that occasions most of the discontent.

As was true for the essays, an interpretation of the students' responses to the questionnaire may emphasize either their positive or their negative aspects. On the one hand, it might be concluded that most students are relatively satisfied with life in school, or at least they *say* they are satisfied. On the other hand, it is equally legitimate to stress the importance of the disgruntled minority. The figures indicate that as much as 20 percent of the students, or about 6 children in every class of 30, have serious misgivings about the value of classroom life.[10] It is possible, in other words, to become either elated or depressed by the questionnaire findings, depending on the perspective from which they are viewed.

Although there is a natural proclivity to stress either the positive or negative aspects of the findings, it is also possible, by combining the results from both the essay and the questionnaire, to argue that the majority of the students do not feel strongly about school life, one way or the other. That is, the majority of the students may "like" school and a smaller number "dislike" it, but one group does not "love" school and the other "hate" it. An interpretation stressing the neutrality of the students' feelings is hinted in Tenenbaum's own conclusions. He states,

> Since the school is an institution in the community, assigned by the community to do a definite task, the child takes it for granted that the institution is doing the task. He is not critical of the institution, he accepts it. This attitude does not make him happy about being a member of the institution. He may be very unhappy within its environs, but, nevertheless, he thinks that the institution is good and desirable and serves worthy ends. The school, it would seem, is a *receiver* of attitudes, *not a creator of them*. The child comes to school with preconceived notions of how to regard school and tries to get and thinks he gets from school what the community expects the school to give.[11]

---

[10] Tenenbaum goes even further and claims that at least 20 percent of the students "are unhappy and maladjusted at school and are ready to quit at any or no pretext." However, the data he presents hardly justify that conclusion. Tenenbaum, "Attitudes of elementary school children to school, teachers, and classmates," p. 134.

[11] Tenenbaum, "Attitudes of elementary school children to school, teachers, and classmates," pp. 140–141.

It is dangerous, of course, to rely too heavily on Tenenbaum's data. His study has obvious limitations that prevent our taking his findings as the final word in estimating how many students like or dislike school. Fortunately, two or three other investigators used procedures roughly comparable with those employed by Tenenbaum and reported findings that can be compared with his.

The questionnaire developed by Tenenbaum was used by another investigator, Sister Josephina, almost twenty years after the first report. The subjects in Sister Josephina's study were 900 students in grades five through eight drawn from nine parochial schools.[12] As in the original design, the students were permitted to respond anonymously to the questionnaire. Although the students did not write an essay on their liking for school, their responses to the single item "I like/do not like school" were tallied (see Table 2).

Table 2 *Student Responses to:*
"I Like/Do Not Like School"[a]

Grade level[b]	BOYS				GIRLS			
	5	6	7	8	5	6	7	8
Like school	82%	70 %	82 %	65 %	88 %	80%	94.6%	83 %
Dislike school	15%	29 %	17.7%	33.3%	11 %	19%	5.3%	16.9%
No reply	2%	.9%	0 %	.9%	.9%	1%	0 %	0 %

[a] Adapted from Sister Josephina, "Study of attitudes in the elementary grades," *Journal of Educational Sociology*, 33:56–60, October 1959.
[b] The exact number of students in each grade was not reported.

The information in Table 2 is roughly equivalent to the summary description of the student essays in Tenenbaum's study, except that here there is no category for "mixed feelings." As before, the overall impression is one of students being satisfied with their school experience, even more satisfied than the students in the original sample seemed to be. Again, however, there is a noticeable percentage of students who admit to disliking school. Moreover, this percentage is about the same as that reported in the earlier study. It seems, then, that the apparent abundance of positive feelings among the parochial students, as compared with the New York public school group, is largely due to the absence of a category in

---

[12] Sister Josephina, "Study of attitudes in the elementary grades" *Journal of Educational Sociology*, 33:56–60, October 1959.

which to register markedly ambivalent feelings. Finally, and again as before, girls are seen to be more pleased with school life than are boys.

With respect to the children's liking of their present teacher, Sister Josephina found an even smaller amount of discontent than did Tenenbaum. The largest number of students expressing a dislike for their present teacher was found in the eighth grade where the relevant percentages were 3.8 and 3.7 for boys and girls respectively. In the lower three grades the percentages for the boys beginning with the fifth grade class were .8, 3.3, and 2.5; for girls the equivalent figures were 1.8, 1.8, and 0. As before, the data support the hypothesis that it is school itself rather than individual teachers that provokes the student's discomfort. Unfortunately, Sister Josephina only reports findings with respect to these two aspects of the students response—their general liking for school and their attitude toward their present teacher. Therefore, other comparisons with Tenenbaum's original study are impossible.

A third study, though even less fully reported than the preceding one, was conducted by L. E. Leipold, the principal of a Minnesota high school.[13] Leipold asked his ninth grade students, 273 in all, to write short essays in response to the query: "Do you like school? Why? Do you dislike school? Why?" His analysis of these essays is summarized in the following table.

Table 3 *Student Responses to the Query:*
"Do You Like School?"[a]

	BOYS[b]	GIRLS	TOTAL
Like school	70 %	81%	75.5%
Dislike school	23.4%	14%	18.5%
No reply	6.6%	5%	5.9%

[a] Adapted from: L. E. Leipold, "Children do like school," *Clearing House,* 31:332–334, February 1957.
[b] The percentages for boys were not given in the report itself but were calculated from the data given for girls and the total group, using the assumption that there was an approximately equal sex division in the sample.

The data from the Minnesota students tell about the same story as that provided by the other two investigators. Again, there is the impression of massive satisfaction, counterbalanced, or at least tempered, by the presence of a disgruntled minority. Again, the girls exceed the boys in the expression of satisfaction.

[13] L. E. Leipold, "Children do like school," *Clearing House,* 31:332–334, February 1957.

Finally, some data recently collected in a suburb of Chicago warrant mention in this overview of student opinion.[14] The data in question, which are part of a larger study of student attitudes, consist of the responses of sixth graders to questions about their life in school. The entire sixth grade (293 students from 11 classes located in nine public schools) of the suburban community participated in the study. The questionnaires were administered in the spring of the year in order to give sufficient time for student opinion to develop and become stable.

Responses to only three of the questions from one of the attitude questionnaires (the *Student Opinion Poll*) are of direct relevance to the topic at hand. Other aspects of the findings will be presented in later sections. The first question deals with the students' attitudes toward the subject matter taught in their classes; the second with the friendliness of the teachers in their school; and the third with their attitudes toward school in general. The specific questions and the percentage of students choosing each response are shown in Table 4.

These findings corroborate, for the most part, those already cited. The percentage of boys whose responses lay on the "negative" side of each question ranged from 20.3 for question #3, to 25.7 for question #1; the percentages of girls taking the "negative" side ranges from 9.7 on question #2 to 18.6 on question #1. Thus, the proportions of discontent are roughly the same as those reported by other investigators. Also, the girls in this study, as in the other studies just described are less critical of their experience than are the boys. In particular, the present group of girls seems to be more satisfied than are the boys with the friendliness of their teachers.

There is one noticeable difference between these results and those reported by Tenenbaum and by Sister Josephina. Both of the latter investigators found students to be less critical of their teachers than of school in general. But, in the responses of the sixth graders presented in Table 4, criticism of teachers, with respect to their friendliness, occurs with about the same frequency as do criticisms of school in general. There is no apparent explanation of this difference, other than the fact that the two earlier studies dealt with the students' general liking for their teacher, whereas question #2 in Table 4 is concerned with a somewhat more specific evaluation.

Before leaving these four sets of data it is well to consider once more what they have told us about students' attitudes toward life in school and to reflect briefly on that information. For these four studies, it appears, contain the only descriptions of grade school

---

[14] The data were collected by Miss Henriette M. Lahaderne while working under my direction.

Table 4 *Student Responses to Three Questions from the* Student Opinion Poll

	BOYS (148)	GIRLS (145)	TOTAL (293)
QUESTION 1. "MOST OF THE SUBJECTS TAUGHT IN THIS SCHOOL ARE			
a. very interesting."	38.5%	42.8%	40.6%
b. above average in interest."	35.1%	38.6%	36.9%
c. below average in interest."	17.6%	13.1%	15.4%
d. dull and uninteresting."	8.1%	5.5%	6.8%
QUESTION 2. "IN GENERAL, TEACHERS IN THIS SCHOOL ARE			
a. very friendly."	41.9%	53.8%	47.8%
b. somewhat friendly."	34.5%	35.9%	35.2%
c. somewhat unfriendly."	16.2%	7.6%	11.9%
d. very unfriendly."	6.1%	2.1%	4.1%
QUESTION 3. "IN GENERAL, MY FEELINGS TOWARD SCHOOL ARE			
a. very favorable—I like it as it is."	35.1%	47.6%	41.3%
b. somewhat favorable—I would like a few changes."	44.6%	40.0%	42.3%
c. somewhat unfavorable—I would like many changes."	12.2%	9.0%	10.6%
d. very unfavorable—I frequently feel that school is pretty much a waste of time."	8.1%	3.4%	5.8%

students' general liking for school that have been reported in the past thirty years.[15] Until more thorough studies are made, these data are all we have to go on when we ask a question such as: "What proportion of students claim to like school?"

As has been pointed out several times in the last few pages, the overall impression provided by the summary statistics contained in Tables 1 through 4 is that students are relatively content with their life in school. Although the proportions differ markedly for boys and for girls, it looks as if about 80 percent of the students in our upper elementary grades would place themselves in the "like"

[15] Many other studies of students' attitudes have been made, but they do not contain normative data with respect to the student's general liking for school and teachers. For the most part research has focused on the *correlates* of students' attitudes—in studies, for example, of college students' ratings of their instructors and course grades—or on the origin and treatment of extreme attitudes in particular students—in studies, for example, of school phobia or of school dropouts.

category if asked to describe themselves as either liking or disliking school. For some people this majority may seem sufficiently large to discourage further inquiry into the matter. Leipold, for example, after presenting the findings summarized in Table 3 adds the following comment on the meaning of the study to him as an educator, "paramount is the conviction that things aren't too bad when four out of five boys and girls frankly admit that they *like school* and can give good reasons."[16] This attitude is likely shared by many others who work with school children. So long as most students seem to like school, "things aren't too bad." We may then ask, "Why bother to probe more deeply?"

The most obvious reason for desiring to probe more deeply is that the proportion of students who claim to dislike school comprise a significant number. If we believe the statistics they would seem to indicate that about one child in five or six students in every average-sized classroom feels a sufficient amount of discomfort to complain about it when given the opportunity. If this figure were similar in all grades and all geographic regions (a big "if" to be sure!) it would mean that when we talk about the child who does not like school we are discussing the problem of some seven million students in our elementary schools alone. Certainly not a number that can be easily dismissed.

Moreover, there is reason to believe that 20 percent may be a conservative estimate of the proportion who privately dislike school. In three of the four studies that have been reviewed the investigators took special precautions to ensure that responses would be treated confidentially and would not be seen by teachers or other school officials. It was hoped that these procedures would increase the honesty of the students' reports. Underlying this belief is the assumption that dishonesty, if it occurred, would bias the reports in the favorable direction. Children, for the most part, like to please adults, and adults, for the most part, like to hear that children are enjoying school. Hopefully, the precautions did work, on the whole, and the students did give an accurate report of their true feelings. But it is unlikely that they worked perfectly. It is probable, therefore, that the actual amount of discontent in the classroom is somewhat greater than the amount revealed in the students' essays and questionnaire responses.

A second reason for wanting to take a closer look at student attitudes than that provided by the studies described so far arises

---

[16] Leipold, p. 334. Leipold's optimism apparently accounts for the slight inaccuracy in his statement. The actual percentage of the students in his study who were found to like school yields a ratio that is closer to three out of four than to four out of five.

from a recognition of the exaggerations contained in a black and white image. When attitudes are dichotomized, as they were in most of the data already discussed, much of their subtlety is lost. When we force students to describe themselves as being either "for" or "against" school, we do obtain a crude picture of their views —one that is easy to recall and to talk about—but this picture is obtained at the cost of ignoring the psychological richness of student opinion. A school is a complex institution, and students are complex creatures. Surely not all youngsters who are "for" school are for it unequivocally. Similarly, not every student whose response is placed in the "nay" column of an opinion poll is eager to have done with everything educational.[17] To understand more fully the information provided by the gross categorization of students' opinion we must move to a consideration of the variability that likely exists on both sides of the like-dislike dichotomy. In other words, we must add gradations of gray to the black and white picture.

A crude indication of the range of dissatisfactions expressed by students is contained in a study conducted at the University of Chicago several years ago.[18] At that time we constructed a 60-item questionnaire, titled the *Student Opinion Poll*, designed to assess a student's satisfaction with his school experience. Each item in the questionnaire consisted of a multiple choice question relating to one of four aspects of school life: teachers, students, curriculum, and classroom practices. Among the responses to each item one alternative contained an expression of complete satisfaction with that particular feature of school life; a student choosing that alternative was given one point. Thus, the possible range of scores was from 0 to 60. When this questionnaire was administered to more than 500 students from grades six through twelve in a well-known private school, the average score was 37.3, and the standard deviation 9.57. In other words, in that advantaged environment the average student (who probably would be placed in the "like school" column if the methods of one of the previously discussed studies were employed) expressed some dissatisfaction on almost half the items.

More recently the same questionnaire was administered to 258

---

[17] After interviewing 52 emotionally disturbed students, each of whom was diagnosed as revealing "a serious school problem" one psychiatrist reported that only ten out of the total group seemed to have "a pure dislike" for school without an admixture of other feelings. See C. E. Schorer, "How emotionally disturbed children view the school," *Exceptional Child*, 27:191–195, December 1960.

[18] Philip W. Jackson and Jacob W. Getzels, "Psychological health and classroom functioning: a study of dissatisfaction with school among adolescents," *Journal of Educational Psychology*, 50:295–300, December 1959.

juniors in a suburban high school.[19] The average score for that group was 29.0. Moreover, the average for the top quartile of those juniors, the group most content with their present school experience, was 39.0, with a standard deviation of 3.45. Thus, even for the most satisfied group some dissatisfaction was expressed on about one-third of the questionnaire items.

Of even greater relevance, because of their bearing on material that has already been discussed, are further results from the study of suburban sixth graders from which the data in Table 4 have been taken. A shortened version of the *Student Opinion Poll*, this one containing 47 items, was administered to that group also and the average scores found to be 25.3 for the boys (with a standard deviation of 8.2), and 29.4 for the girls (with a standard deviation of 8.2). The average student in this sample, it will be recalled, clearly declared himself as being "for" school and "for" his teachers. Yet he proceeded, when questioned more fully, to reveal many areas of school life with which he was not completely satisfied.

Obviously, the opposing argument could be applied by compiling corresponding statistics for the smaller group of students who describe themselves as being against school. That is, there are doubtlessly several things about school with which the disgruntled student is perfectly content. But the point has probably been made with sufficient force by focusing on the "satisfied" group. Although they were not originally collected for this purpose, and therefore leave much to be desired, the data that have been presented should be enough to disturb the complacency of educators who maintain their calm by pointing to the fact that "most students like school." Most do like school, but not entirely.

Another way of revealing some of the subtleties of student attitudes is by calling attention to the ambiguities, if not downright contradictions, occasionally revealed in students' opinion of life in school. In a study of 1000 high school students, for example, 91 percent of the sample agreed that "teachers as a whole are friendly."[20] Yet 40.5 percent of the same group of students agreed that "teachers are glad when 3:00 o'clock comes so the brats can go home." About 21 percent of these students, who saw teachers as being so friendly, also said "yes" to the statement: "The facial expression of most teachers is distressing." An additional 26 percent were "undecided." Perhaps there is no logical contradiction revealed here, but these results are at least a bit puzzling.

---

[19] Richard C. Diedrich, "Teacher perceptions as related to teacher-student similarity and student satisfaction with school," Unpublished Ph.D. thesis, University of Chicago, March 1966.

[20] Paul R. Cobb, "High school seniors' attitudes toward teachers and the teaching profession," *Bulletin of the National Association of Secondary-School Principals*, 36:140–144, January 1952.

A more subtle kind of ambiguity is revealed (but not commented upon) in a survey of the attitudes of 314 fifth grade students in Tennessee.[21] The investigator, Myrtle G. Dye, compared the opinions of two groups of students—one comprised of "gifted" youngsters (taken from the top ten percent of the school population on the basis of IQ test performance), the other of "average" youngsters (scores between the 45th and the 55th percentiles on the same IQ tests)—on a 60-item questionnaire dealing with school life. Among the average group 97 percent of the boys and 94 percent of the girls were found to be "happy" in school. Equivalent figures for the gifted group were 79 and 87 percent. Yet 25 percent of the boys thought the school day could be shortened and when asked to nominate their favorite grade from among those they had experienced so far, about 40 percent of the total group chose one of their previous grades rather than the one in which they were presently enrolled.

In other words, although almost all of the Tennessee fifth graders were judged to be "happy" with their present classroom experience, about a quarter of the boys could do with less of it, and close to half of the students could remember a time when they had been more satisfied with school life. As one considers these contrasts it seems as if many of the students were trying to say something like, "School is fine—but it could be better."

Usually when students are found to like their school and their teachers it is assumed that they are "happy" while in the classroom. But the equating of "liking" with "happiness" is unnecessary and serves only to reinforce the simplistic view of student attitudes that we are attempting here to dispel. Not all children who like school can be described as being continually happy while there. Some consideration of the negative feelings that might be engendered by the classroom experience is appropriate, therefore, as we seek to move beyond a dichotomous pro-or-con view of student attitudes.

If a sizeable proportion of high school seniors find their teacher's facial expression distressing, as the study described a few paragraphs ago would seem to indicate, how distressing are teachers' facial expressions and their general actions to younger children? A partial answer to this question is provided in one of the few studies to examine the school attitudes of students in the primary grades.[22]

Interviews were conducted with 128 children from four schools in a large suburban system. The sample contained 32 students in each of four grades: kindergarten, first, second, and third. The

[21] Myrtle G. Dye, "Attitudes of gifted children toward school," *Educational Administration and Supervision*, 42:301–308, 1956.

[22] Lee B. Sechrest, "Motivation in school of young children: some interview data," *Journal of Experimental Education*, 30:327–335, June 1962.

children were asked many questions about their life in school and the investigator reports that, on the whole, they seemed to be enjoying school very much. But when they were asked: "What does your teacher do that frightens or scares you?" about 44 percent of the students were able to name some behavior of the teacher that upset them ("yelling and making loud noises" was mentioned most frequently).

Another study in which school-related feelings are prominent is one in which a 53-item inventory, cataloging some of the things about which children might worry, was administered to "several hundred" fifth- and sixth-grade students in New York City.[23] The matter about which the children admitted worrying the most was "failing a test." Among the boys, 29 percent described themselves as being afflicted with such a worry "often," 59 percent answered "sometimes," and 12 percent said "never." The equivalent figures for girls were 37 percent "often," 54 percent "sometimes," and 9 percent "never."

It is possible, of course, that such worries may be less frequent today than they were in 1940 when the study was made, but it should be remembered that these concerns were revealed in the same year, in the same school system, and at approximately the same grade level, at which Tenenbaum was conducting his studies, which, as we have seen, reported that about 20 percent of the students disliked school. A reasonable conclusion would seem to be that many who like school also worry about it.

The existence of negative feelings among students who are basically satisfied with school life is dramatically portrayed in data collected in two of our Chicago studies.[24, 25] In the first of these investigations (Study I) a group of "satisfied" students was identified on the basis of their responses to the *Student Opinion Poll*.[26] A student was classified as "satisfied" if his score on the instrument was at least one and a half standard deviations above the mean of the entire student body. Forty-five students were selected in this manner from among the 531 students who responded to the questionnaire. The students in this study were enrolled in grades six through twelve in a Midwestern private school.

The second investigation (Study II) was conducted in a public high school in the Midwest. All students in the junior class of that school participated in the study. The "satisfied" group, which con-

[23] R. Pintner and J. Lev, "Worries of school children," *Pedagogical Seminary*, **56**:67–76, March 1940.

[24] Jackson and Getzels.

[25] Philip W. Jackson and Richard C. Diedrich, "The evaluation of school experiences: a study of satisfied and dissatisfied students," Mimeographed, 1965.

[26] See p. 55 for a brief description of this questionnaire.

sisted of 69 students, was selected by the same procedure as that employed in Study I.

In both studies all of the students responded to a checklist, which consisted of 25 adjectives. Each student was asked to choose the six adjectives that best described his characteristic feelings while attending classes in particular school subjects. The list contained 12 "positive" adjectives (for example, confident, happy, eager) and 12 "negative" adjectives (for example, bored, restless, angry). The responses of the "satisfied" students to the negative adjectives are summarized in Table 5.[27]

Table 5 *Negative Adjectives Chosen by "Satisfied Students" Asked to Describe Classroom Feelings*

ADJECTIVE[a]	TIMES CHOSEN			
	Boys		Girls	
	Study I (25)	Study II (34)	Study I (20)	Study II (35)
Bored	13	26	13	25
Uncertain	21	25	13	26
Dull	16	24	9	25
Restless	15	20	9	26
Inadequate	16	20	7	24
Unnoticed	5	16	4	15
Unhelped	8	16	6	17
Ignorant	13	15	3	15
Angry	4	14	4	14
Restrained	2	11	3	10
Misunderstood	5	11	2	15
Rejected	3	9	0	10

[a] Adjectives have been ordered in this Table on the basis of the ranking of the responses of boys in Study II.

The data in Table 5 tell a clear story. In both studies students who were apparently satisfied with school made frequent use of negative adjectives when asked to describe their *typical* classroom feelings. In Study I, for example, half of the boys and more than half of the girls claimed that a feeling of boredom was typical in

[27] In both studies groups of *dis*satisfied students were also identified. These groups, as might be expected, chose negative adjectives to describe their classroom feelings much more frequently than did the students whose responses are summarized in Table 5. The complete reports of these two studies contain comparisons of the satisfied and the dissatisfied students.

some of their classes. In Study II the proportion of students reporting boredom and other negative feelings is even higher than it is for the private school group.

Here then is further evidence of the complexity of student attitudes toward school. As we look more closely at these phenomena the extremes of satisfaction and dissatisfaction draw closer together. Gradually the black and white picture changes to gray.

When Tenenbaum analyzed the essays from his sample of students he commented, the reader will recall, on the relative absence of expressions of strong feeling. He talked about the frequency of "stereotyped" responses that followed "conventional patterns." Having obtained a glimpse of some of the ambiguities and contradictions that characterize student attitudes, we are now in a better position to appreciate the significance of Tenenbaum's remarks.

The number of students who become ecstatic when the school bell rings and who remain that way all day is probably very small, as is the number who sit in the back of the room and grind their teeth in anger from opening exercises to dismissal. One way of interpreting the data we have reviewed so far is to suggest that most students do not feel too strongly about their classroom experience, one way or the other.[28]

This fact, if we can assume for the moment that it is a fact, must be considered in the light of what has already been said about the classroom environment and the nature of the child's participation in that environment. Just as extreme feeling is sometimes occasioned by what happens to a person, so, too, is the absence of extreme feeling. Apathy and neutrality are no less adaptive than are joy and hate, and to some extent might even be considered more so. Therefore, it is reasonable to inquire into the causes behind the seemingly restricted range of student feelings. Although this task will occupy us in several of the chapters that lie ahead, at least a beginning may be made here.

First, as we have already seen, reactions to school life are considerably varied. Students tend to like some aspects of that life and dislike others. Moreover, as we have also seen, even the most satisfied students have their complaints, and the least satisfied their pleasures. These combinations of feeling, which, when summed, yield a general attitude of ambivalence, arise in part from the inevitable mismatch between individual desires and institutional

---

[28] It is possible that attitudes toward school are not constant throughout the year. In the beginning and ending of the term, for example, school might be approached with greater eagerness than is true the rest of the year. Clarence Darrow once remarked, "School had at least two days that made us as happy as children could well be. One was the first day of the term, and the other was the last."

goals. The needs and interests of the child as he experiences them subjectively are often not consonant with his needs as perceived by the institution, or with the needs of others who are also served by the institution. This means, in short, that sometimes he will want to do the tasks assigned him and other times he will not. Under the one condition he should experience a certain amount of pleasure, and under the other a certain amount of pain.

A second reason why certain kinds of extreme feelings may not appear too frequently in the classroom is that students must attend whether they want to or not. The fact of compulsory attendance likely does much to reduce outbursts of protests and complaints. When the bonds are sufficiently secure, resistance becomes futile. If school is inevitable, better relax and accept it.

A third, and perhaps the most important, reason why attitudes toward school tend toward neutrality is that school becomes "old hat" for most students. Shortly after his initiation into the institution the young child develops an understanding of what school is like and in the years that follow his initial views are not modified radically. Patterns of social interaction remain about the same throughout the grades and the physical environment remains very much the same as he moves from one room to the next in the same school building. The content of the work may change in each successive grade but, essentially, arithmetic is arithmetic and spelling is spelling. This year's teacher may be nicer than last year's but both are teachers and the student's relationship with both is a highly standardized flowering of stable role expectations. After the first few thousand hours of attendance (and possibly long before then) the global experience of being in school probably holds few surprises for most students. This is not to say, of course, that surprising events do not take place in the classroom. Many otherwise dull days are brightened by unexpected happenings, and many teachers do their best to inject novelty into the daily lesson. But the excitement of school, its sharp disappointments as well as its joys, is contained in colorful interludes that interrupt, rather than characterize, the normal flow of events.

II

In the first section we saw how students' attitudes toward classroom events are really more complex than is implied by the conventional practice of asking youngsters whether or not they like school, even though answers to that standard query often provide useful information. This complexity derives from two related aspects of student opinion. First is the admixture, to be found in some, of strong likes and dislikes and of contradictory attitudes toward specific features of school life. Second, and perhaps partially as a consequence of these contradictory elements, there seems to develop, in some students, a separation between their feelings and the daily business of classroom life. For these students (and no one seems to know how many fit this description) school is just another of life's inevitabilities toward which is adopted in I-can-take-it-or-leave-it attitude.

Yet, despite this complexity, stable differences do exist among students in their over-all liking for school. It is evident, for example, that girls react more positively to school than do boys. We know, further, that thousands of students dislike school sufficiently to withdraw from it at the earliest opportunity, while others look forward with regret to the end of their days in school. The purpose of this section is to examine some of the educational consequences of these differences, beginning with the simple question of how visible they are to teachers.

Certain aspects of the teacher's perception of students' attitudes are almost too obvious to bear comment and, therefore, can be dispensed with rather quickly. It seems clear, for example, that extreme forms of student opinion are often visible to even the most insensitive teacher. When a student openly declares his distaste for school or does it only slightly more subtly by indicating his desire to quit school, the need for guesswork on the part of the teacher is eliminated.

Most teachers are equally aware, in all probability, of differences in the reactions of the entire class to specific parts of the school program. Most would agree, for example, that their students prefer physical education to spelling, or watching a movie to completing an exercise in an arithmetic workbook. No teacher in the lower grades can fail to miss the groans of disappointment that erupt when she announces that recess will be held indoors, or the shouts of delight that accompany the announcement of an early dismissal. In sum, almost all teachers are surely aware of gross differences in their students' reactions to recurring classroom events.

When it comes to the more subtle and individual aspects of student opinion, however, less is known of their visibility to the teacher. It is safe to say that the teacher typically does not know all there is to know about his students' attitudes toward school, but this does not say much. In order to say more some kind of empirical evidence is called for.

One way of considering the visibility of students' attitudes is to ask whether teachers can predict how their students will respond to a school attitude questionnaire. Naturally, no teacher could accurately predict his students' responses to each and every item on such a questionnaire. No one would expect him to be that perceptive. A more reasonable task might be to ask for a categorization of the students into groups representing varying levels of satisfaction. The teacher might be asked, in other words, to identify the most and least satisfied students in his room, allowing several students in each category, and this classification could be matched against a similar one based on the students' actual responses to questions about their school attitudes. This approach was used in the study of the sixth graders described in the last section (see pp. 52), and the results, while not highly generalizable, are sufficiently interesting to warrant a detailed discussion.

Two hundred and ninety-three students from eleven classrooms (all of the sixth grade rooms in the public school system of a suburban community) responded to a 47-item questionnaire designed to assess attitudes toward school.[29] The teacher in each classroom was shown sample items from the questionnaire and was given a brief description of its avowed purpose. He was then asked to predict, in a relative way, how each of his students might respond to such a set of questions.[30]

When expressed as a correlation coefficient the overall relationship between the teachers' ratings and the students' responses to the questionnaire yielded a value of .35. This single statistic does not provide much information, but it does indicate that the accuracy of the teachers' predictions was decidedly better than chance. The same statistic also indicates, of course, that these teachers were far from perfect in their estimates. Apparently some aspects of students' attitudes are visible to teachers and others are not. To learn more about this partial visibility we must undertake a more refined analysis.

A second way of depicting the gross character of the relationship between the teachers' predictions and the actual responses of the students is by applying the concepts of "hits" and "misses" in

---

[29] The questionnaire was a revised version of the *Student Opinion Poll* described on page 55.

[30] The procedure for obtaining the ratings was as follows: Each teacher was presented with an alphabetized list of his students. He was asked, first, to divide the group into thirds by classifying his students into three levels of satisfaction: "most," "average," and "least." He was then asked to identify from within the groups labelled "most" and "least" a smaller number of students (one fourth of each group) who seemed to represent extreme positions ("very satisfied" and "very dissatisfied"). Thus, each student's attitudes was described by his teacher as falling into one of five categories. In each classroom the approximate proportion of students in the five categories were: 1/12, 1/4, 1/3, 1/4, 1/12. When the ratings were treated quantitatively the values 15, 12, 10, 8, and 5 were assigned to the five groupings, the highest number being used to represent the students whom the teacher described as "very satisfied."

describing the accuracy of the teachers' judgments. "Hits," as the term implies, are instances in which the teacher guessed correctly and "misses" are instances in which he guessed incorrectly. What is meant by a correct or incorrect guess needs definition, of course, because the judgments (teachers' placement of the students into five categories) and the qualities being judged (students' total scores on a school opinionnaire) are not expressed in the same units.

In order to make the definition as unambiguous as possible, and, thus, to increase the ease with which the findings can be discussed, certain of the complexities in the raw data have been ignored or eliminated. First, the students who themselves expressed a middling attitude toward school, and whose scores therefore might be the most difficult to interpret, were withdrawn from the sample.[31] Thus, in the analysis that follows we are concerned only with the teachers' judgments of those students who have expressed rather clear-cut opinions, either positive or negative, of what life in school is like. Second, the teachers' judgments have also been simplified by reducing, from five to three, the number of categories into which the predictions were grouped. This reduction was accomplished by ignoring the labels "most" and "least" attached to the extreme groups and by treating the entire sample as if the students had been classified into three groups, "satisfied," "average," or "dissatisfied," with approximately one-third of the sample in each.

A teacher's judgment was considered a "hit" if he classified as "satisfied" a student whose score on the *Student Opinion Poll* was at least one-half a standard deviation *above* the mean of the total sample, or as "dissatisfied," a student whose score was at least one-half a standard deviation *below* the mean. A "miss" was defined as occurring when the teacher judged the student to be in the top or bottom third of the class but his actual score in the questionnaire placed him in the opposite group. The teacher's judgment was considered "uncertain" when he placed into the "average" category any of the students whose scores on the opinionnaire were more than one-half of a standard deviation away from the mean. Applying these definitions, we would expect the teachers' judgments to be classified, by chance alone, as one-third "hits," one-third "misses,"

---

[31] The withdrawn group was composed of students whose scores on the *Student Opinion Poll* were within one-half of a standard deviation from the mean of the total sample. In a normally distributed population this procedure would have eliminated approximately 38 percent of the sample, leaving 31 percent in each of the two remaining groups. However, because scores on the *Student Opinion Poll* were slightly skewed toward the positive end of the scale, the actual percentage of students in the withdrawn group was 36.6, leaving 34.6 percent in the "satisfied" category and 28.8 percent in the "dissatisfied" category.

and one-third "uncertain."[32] Deviations from these chance expectations were tested to see if they were statistically significant and the results, along with the actual numbers and percentages in each category, are presented in Table 6.

Table 6   *Accuracy of Teachers' Predictions of Students' Attitudes*

PREDICTIONS	STUDENTS' ATTITUDES			
	"Satisfied"		"Dissatisfied"	
	N	%	N	%
Hits	53	52.5	30	35.7
Uncertain	25	24.8	36	42.8
Misses	23	22.7	18	21.5
	$x^2 = 16.7$[a]		$x^2 = 6.00$[b]	

[a] Significant at the .01 level.
[b] Significant at the .05 level.

The data in Table 6 confirm the information contained in the correlation coefficient for the total group (that is, the teachers can predict student attitudes with a greater-than-chance accuracy). But a refinement can now be added to that general conclusion. Apparently the teachers can identify "satisfied" students more accurately than they can "dissatisfied" ones. Also, the reduced accuracy with the "dissatisfied" group does not arise from a larger proportion of outright "misses" with these students, rather the teachers are less likely to judge these students as fitting either extreme. In other words, the teachers were no more likely to misjudge one group than the other but the opinions of the satisfied students were somehow more visible than were the opinions of the dissatisfied students.

---

[32] This is so because the teachers are required to classify their total group of students by thirds, into "satisfied," "average," and "dissatisfied" categories. Thus, if the students whose score on the Student Opinion Poll caused them to be classified as "satisfied" had been randomly arranged by the teachers, one-third of them would be called "satisfied" and, thus, would be counted as "uncertain;" and one-third would be called "dissatisfied" and would be counted as "misses." The same reasoning also applies to those students whose score on the opinionnaire caused them to be labeled "dissatisfied." The fact that the "satisfied" students (by SOP scores) comprise a little more than one-third (34.6 percent) of the sample and the "dissatisfied" a little less than one-third (28.8 percent), means that it is impossible for the teachers to achieve perfect accuracy (100 percent "hits") or perfect inaccuracy (100 percent "misses") in their predictions. But this limitation is relatively unimportant because the observed degrees of accuracy never approach these extremes.

It is naturally unwise to move from these findings, based on such a small number of students in a single school grade, to the general conclusion that student satisfaction is more visible to the teacher than is student dissatisfaction. But the teachers' perception of these sixth graders does seem to make sense in the light of what we know about human behavior in general. In any social situation dissatisfaction is potentially threatening to the well-being of the group and the continued participation of its members. Moreover, the expression of dissatisfaction is often perceived as an affront by the person or persons in charge of the gathering. The social affront implied in an expression of dissatisfaction explains why we compliment our hostess when we leave the party and keep to ourselves any unpleasant feelings that might have been aroused by the experience. We behave in this way not just to conform to social convention but to ensure our social survival.

In the classroom the damage that might be done by the expression of dissatisfaction is magnified by the power of the sanctions available to the teacher. Unlike the hostess, who might only give her critic an icy stare and fail to invite him back, the teacher is in a position to respond to criticism in ways that are at once more enduring and more painful. The fact that most teachers would not use their authority to squelch honest criticism does little to reduce the fact of that authority and its implicit threat to would-be critics. The dominant strategy of "pleasing the teacher" likely involves more than handing in homework papers on time or keeping in line on the way to the playground; it also involves being vocal about satisfactions while keeping silent about many of the discomforts engendered by classroom life.

If the fact that girls seem happier with their school experience than do boys were recognized by teachers, the job of predicting student attitudes should become somewhat easier when both boys and girls are to be judged than when either sex is considered separately. In other words, when all of his students are considered together a teacher might increase the accuracy of his predictions by consistently giving slightly higher ratings to girls. This effect can be observed in the correlational data obtained from the study under discussion. It will be recalled that the relationship between the teachers' ratings and the actual responses of the total student sample yielded a coefficient of .35. That same relationship, when computed separately for the two sexes is .28 for boys and .28 for girls. The decrease in the size of the coefficients when the sexes are considered separately is not great, but it does call attention to the slight advantage that comes from knowing that girls, on the whole, express more positive attitudes toward school than do boys.

The fact that the coefficients between teachers' predictions and students' scores on the *Student Opinion Poll* are the same size for both boys and girls makes it appear that the teachers can predict the attitudes of both groups with equal accuracy. However, this conclusion, like the one about the general relationship, can be refined somewhat if we turn again to an analysis of the "hits" and "misses" made by the teachers in their estimates of students' attitudes, this time focusing on sex differences in the accuracy of the teachers' judgment. As before, the students under consideration include only those whose expressed attitudes were relatively extreme. The data are summarized in Table 7.

Table 7 *Accuracy of Teachers' Predictions Related to Sex of Students*

PREDICTIONS	BOYS' ATTITUDES				GIRLS' ATTITUDES			
	"Satisfied"		"Dissatisfied"		"Satisfied"		"Dissatisfied"	
	N	%	N	%	N	%	N	%
Hits	11	35.4	24	46.1	42	60.0	6	18.7
Uncertain	10	32.3	21	40.4	15	21.4	15	46.9
Misses	10	32.3	7	13.5	13	18.6	11	34.4
	$\chi^2 = .06$		$\chi^2 = 9.5^a$		$\chi^2 = 22.48^a$		$\chi^2 = 3.81$	

[a] Significant at the .01 level.

Table 7 reveals a striking sex difference in the accuracy of the teachers' predictions. This difference, however, is not the simple one of teachers being more accurate in predicting the scores of girls than of boys, or vice versa. It involves the quality of the attitude as well as the sex of the person holding it. The teachers seem to perceive two of the groups—the "satisfied" girls and the "dissatisfied" boys—more accurately than they do the other two. In other words, the girls who seem to be the happiest with their school experience and the boys who seem to be the least happy are the ones the teachers have the least difficulty in assessing, whereas the attitudes of the contrasting groups of "satisfied" boys and "dissatisfied" girls are not predicted with greater than chance accuracy by the teachers.

Naturally, we must be cautious in making inferences from these findings. But it is important to point out that they do make sense in the light of what is already known about sex differences and classroom characteristics. There is some evidence, for example, that dissatisfied boys are more willing to criticize persons in positions of authority than are dissatisfied girls. In one of the studies mentioned earlier it was found that when students were asked to describe their typical classroom feelings, the dissatisfied boys, more frequently than the dissatisfied girls, used "extrapunitive" adjectives—words that placed the blame for the students' condition on others (for example, misunderstood, rejected). The dissatisfied girls, in contrast, tended to employ more "intropunitive" adjectives—words that placed the blame for the student's condition on the student herself (for example, inadequate, ignorant).[33] If a similar phenomenon were in operation in the sixth grade classrooms under discussion—that is, if dissatisfied boys were more willing to express criticism toward authorities—it would help to explain why such boys might be more visible to the teacher than are dissatisfied girls.

The reason why the satisfied girls are more visible to the teachers than are the satisfied boys is not so easily apparent. Perhaps girls are just more willing to give direct expression to their satisfactions than are boys. Or perhaps the girls who are particularly pleased with school are more likely than are boys to express their feelings to their teachers indirectly by volunteering to help on classroom chores (most of which are feminine in character) or by preferring to stay with or near the teacher when alternative activities are available (on the playground, before and after school).[34]

Somewhat unexpectedly, another variable, the IQ scores of students, was found to be related to the accuracy of the teachers' predictions. As a group these teachers were noticeably more accurate in estimating the attitudes of students with high IQ than they were in estimating the attitudes of the students with low IQ. For the group of sixth graders whose IQ scores were 120 and above (49 students in all) the correlation between the teachers' predictions and actual scores on the *Student Opinion Poll* was .56; for those whose IQ scores were between 90 and 119 (193 students) the corresponding correlation was .30; finally, for those with scores below 90 (46 students) the correlation was .11. When translated into the language of "hits" and "misses" this set of relationships yields the figures presented in Table 8.

Notice that the data in Table 8 refer to the *accuracy* of the teachers' judgments and not to the *type* of attitudes they ascribe to each of the three IQ groups. Apparently something happened to make the attitudes of the high and middle IQ groups visible to the

---

[33] Jackson and Getzels.

[34] The possibility that the sex of the teacher may be related to the perception of student attitude was considered, but no evidence was found to support it. Four of the eleven sixth grade teachers were men, and so far as could be determined the correlations between their predictions of student attitudes and the responses of their students did not differ systematically (even when examined separately for boys and girls) from those obtained from the women teachers.

Table 8 *Accuracy of Teachers' Predictions Related to IQ of Students*

PREDICTIONS	IQ 89 AND BELOW		IQ 90–119		IQ 120 AND ABOVE	
	N	%	N	%	N	%
Hits	10	34.5	55	44.4	17	54.9
Uncertain	9	31.0	44	35.5	8	25.8
Misses	10	34.5	25	20.2	6	19.3
	$x^2 = .07$		$x^2 = 11.14$[a]		$x^2 = 6.66$[b]	

[a] Significant at the .01 level.
[b] Significant at the .05 level.

teachers and the attitudes of the low IQ group obscure. Without further information we can do no more than speculate on a few of the possible causes of this finding. One possibility is that the greater verbal fluency of the high IQ students allows them to communicate their views on school matters more clearly than can their classmates who lack these verbal skills. It is also possible that the teacher interacts more frequently with the high and middle IQ student and, thus, has a greater exposure to their views on school matters than those of the low IQ students. Again, perhaps the high IQ students are more likely to assume positions of leadership in the class, and, thus, might be called upon more frequently than the low IQ students to make their views public. Of course these conditions described in the three explanations are not mutually exclusive. Moreover, all three of these possibilities (and others not mentioned here) may be operating simultaneously. To this point the findings from the sixth-grade classes may be summarized as follows. In general, satisfaction seems to be more visible to the teachers than is dissatisfaction, satisfied girls and dissatisfied boys tend to be particularly salient, and students whose IQ scores are average or above manage in some way to communicate their attitudes more clearly to teachers than do students with low IQ's. These findings are evident when the total group of students and teachers is considered, but they cannot always be seen clearly in the results from each classroom. Some teachers seem to be plainly better than others in estimating how their students will respond to a school attitude questionnaire. Moreover, differences in the accuracy of individual teachers does not seem to be accounted for by differences in the composition of their class, at least not with respect to the students' sex, intelligence level, or degree of satisfaction with school. This conclusion is derived from the data presented in Table 9.

Table 9 · *Accuracy of Individual Teachers' Prediction of Student Attitudes*

CLASS	r^a BETWEEN PREDICTED AND ACTUAL SOP SCORE	CLASSROOM CHARACTERISTICS				
		Sex of Teacher	Boys	Girls	Average IQ	SOP[b] Score
1	.10	F	12	19	101.1	28.71
2	.38	F	18	12	109.0	31.00
3	.52	F	13	15	105.1	25.43
4	.00	F	12	10	98.0	28.27
5	.45	M	20	8	107.4	27.96
6	.30	F	10	19	112.5	21.44
7	.56	F	11	13	93.5	24.67
8	.42	M	18	10	97.0	28.11
9	.46	M	11	19	99.3	28.33
10	−.51	F	6	4	109.9	28.90
11	.26	M	17	16	106.2	28.36

[a] Pearson correlation coefficient.
[b] *Student Opinion Poll.*

The data in Table 9 support two generalizations. First, there is considerable variability from teacher to teacher in the accuracy of their predictions. The estimates from the teacher in class 4, as an instance, bear no systematic relation to the actual responses of her students, whereas those from the teacher in class 7 parallel, at least roughly, her students' scores on the questionnaire.[35] Second, the variability among the teachers does not seem to be related in any systematic way to the variability of the classes on those characteristics that have already been discussed. That is, the teachers who seem to have done relatively well in estimating their students' attitudes do not seem to owe their success to the fact that their classes contained an unequal sex distribution or large numbers of very bright students, or students who were unusually satisfied with school. Why some teachers do seem to do better than others on this task is a question yet to be answered.

Thus far the discussion has focused on the conditions that *enhance* the visibility of student attitudes. But it is also possible to

---

[35] The correlation obtained with the data from class 10 would obviously provide an even more dramatic example of the differences among the teachers. However, that coefficient is based on such a small number of students that it seems unwise to emphasize its atypicality.

focus on a consideration of the conditions that *cloud* the teacher's vision. Instead of asking, as we have been, what student qualities are associated with an unusual proportion of "hits" for these teachers, we might change the question to: What student qualities are associated with "misses"?

The findings already presented with respect to the IQ levels of students provide a useful clue in answering this last question. The material in Table 8, it will be recalled, indicated that the attitudes of students with high IQ's seemed to be more visible to the teachers than did corresponding attitudes among students with low IQ's. In other words, the teachers made fewer "misses" with the high IQ group. But what the figures in Table 8 do not reveal is that the teachers' "misses" with both the high and the low IQ groups are of a special sort.

All 10 of the "misses" in the low IQ group involved students who seemed to be satisfied with school, but whom the teachers perceived as dissatisfied. In contrast, all six of the "misses" in the high IQ group involved students who seemed to be dissatisfied with school but whom the teachers perceived as satisfied. In other words, the teachers tended to overestimate the amount of satisfaction to be found among the students with high IQ's and the amount of dissatisfaction to be found among the students with low IQ's. The teachers' "misses" in the middle IQ group were almost equally divided between "satisfied" students whom the teachers predicted would be dissatisfied (12 of the 25 "misses") and "dissatisfied" students whom the teachers predicted would be satisfied (the remaining 13).

This apparent bias in the teachers' judgments raises the question of whether these teachers are basing their estimates of student attitudes largely upon evidence of the student's intellectual prowess or possibly on related evidence of the students success in mastering academic objectives. Perhaps the teachers' beliefs, if summarized in the form of an adage, would be expressed in something like: "The student who *does* well in school *thinks* well of school." A hint of this kind of belief is revealed in Table 10 in which are shown the correlations between the teachers' estimates of student attitudes and the students' scores on IQ and achievement tests. The correlations between the teacher's estimates and the students' scores on the *Student Opinion Poll,* which have already been presented, are included in Table 10 for purposes of comparison.

In the judgment of these sixth-grade teachers the brighter students, who are also among the top performers on achievement tests, are the ones who appear to be the most satisfied with school. Indeed, the teachers' estimates of their students responses to a school opinionnaire turn out to be more closely related to the

Table 10 *Correlations between Teachers' Estimates of Students' Attitudes and Measures of Intellectual Performance*

	IQ	ACHIEVEMENT TESTS			SOP SCORES
		Reading	Language Arts	Arithmetic	
Boys (148)	.44	.49	.51	.45	.28
Girls (144)	.39	.36	.37	.31	.27

students' academic standing than to their actual responses to the questionnaire. This effect is more pronounced for boys than for girls, but it is evident for both sexes. According to these teachers, "good" students are the ones who appear to be satisfied with school and "poor" students are the ones who appear to be dissatisfied.

But are the teachers really in error? After all, there does seem to be something logically compelling about the conjoining of success and satisfaction. Perhaps the better students really are more content with what goes on in the classroom, and the poorer students more discontent. Perhaps the teachers have merely overestimated the extent to which this is so. This possibility requires an examination of the relationship between academic achievement, on the one hand, and attitudes toward school, on the other. It is to this important topic that we now turn.

III

At least two lines of reasoning can be used to arrive at the expectation that scholastic success and positive attitudes toward school go hand in hand. Both are common enough to have been heard several times by most readers, but because each contains some unwarranted assumptions to be discussed later in this chapter, an overview of both arguments is presented here.

The first set of expectations in support of a success-satisfaction linkage derives from the well-known fact that rewards tend to arouse positive feelings and punishments, negative feelings. People are usually happy when the good things of life come their way and unhappy when their good fortune ceases. Indeed, the connection between rewards and punishments, on the one hand, and particular feeling states, on the other, is so compellingly evident that Edward L. Thorndike, in his pioneering studies of learning, adopted the terms "satisfiers" and "annoyers" to refer to the conditions that led to the strengthening or weakening of response tendencies. When Thorndike wanted an animal to repeat an act he arranged to have that behavior followed by a "satisfier" and when the goal was to eliminate the behavior, "annoyers" were used. Although present-day psychologists might prefer more neutral terms, such as "positive reinforcement" or "negative reinforcement," no one seriously questions the aptness of Thorndike's language for describing what happens in higher organisms, and particularly in man, when rewards and punishments are introduced.

Not only is reward satisfying and punishment annoying, but (the argument continues) after a time the settings in which one or the other of these conditions is continually experienced begins to engender the associated feeling on its own. In other words, the attitudinal components of rewards and punishments tend to rub off, as it were, and become attached to the situations in which they are administered. For example, the sights and smells of the dentist's office become almost as disquieting as the drill itself for many people.

The application of this line of reasoning to educational affairs is easily made. Obviously, schools are places in which rewards and punishments are administered in abundance. Smiles, compliments, special privileges, good grades, and high scores on tests are occasioned by certain kinds of classroom behavior. Frowns, scoldings, deprivations, poor grades, and low scores on tests are occasioned by other kinds. Further, these satisfying and annoying experiences are not evenly distributed among the students but, instead, tend to be concentrated in both kind and number. Some students become accustomed to receiving the classroom rewards; others to receiving the classroom punishments. Paralleling what was said about human behavior in general we would expect rewarded students to develop, over time, a genuine liking for schools and the process of schooling. Similarly, we would expect students who typically are not rewarded and who frequently may even be punished, to become more or less dissatisfied with life in the classroom. Hence the general expectation: scholastic success will be associated with positive attitudes toward school.

A second line of reasoning leading to the same conclusion is a derivative of the age-old observation that the best milk comes from contented cows. In this case the direction of causality between effective performance and the feelings of the performer is the reverse of that implied in the first argument. Here the emphasis is on the contribution of positive feelings to the worker's output, rather than vice versa.

The effectiveness of performance, so the argument goes, is at least partially dependent on the motivation of the performer. The man who does not want to work often does not do his job as well as does the man who approaches his task enthusiastically, or at least willingly. The ability to concentrate and the willingness to endure petty annoyances—two conditions that contribute substantially to success on complicated tasks—seem to be derived in large measure from the general predisposition of the worker. In most important tasks it is impossible to succeed without trying, and trying, as we know, involves a complicated engagement of desires, attitudes, and other motivational constructs. Moreover, these motivational components are not developed *sui generis* in each work situation but, instead, contain pervasive and enduring elements that are brought to the situation by the worker. The person who enters a situation feeling generally satisfied with the condition in which he finds himself is more likely than is his disgruntled companion to cope successfully with the specific demands of that situation.

The translation of this argument into the language of classroom events is, as before, a simple matter. Schoolwork, like tasks encountered in other settings, requires concentration and effort. To succeed in the classroom a student must continually *try* to succeed and this implies, in turn, that he must *want* to try. Now we might expect that those students who are the most eager to cope with specific learning tasks are also the ones who respond most positively to the general experience of schooling. In other words, the youngsters who are the most satisfied with school, other things equal, ought to be among the ones who are the most successful in the classroom.

Thus by two separate paths it is possible to arrive at the same conclusion: scholastic success and satisfaction with school ought to be positively related. Moreover, although they have been treated separately, the two arguments by which this conclusion has been reached can also be shown to reinforce each other. Scholastic success, in this view, may be thought to engender positive attitudes toward school, which, in turn, enhance the possibility of further success, and so on. And of course the same cyclic process is expected to operate at the opposite end of the continuum where the outcomes are not so pleasant. Thus, at the same time as the successful student is pictured soaring on to new heights of achievement with a smile on his face, the failing student is seen as sinking further and further down in the academic heap, his frown deepening as he descends.

As often happens, however,—largely because the logical and the psychological are seldom the same—things do not work in real life quite the way the armchair theorist would like them to. The logically anticipated relationship between students' attitudes toward school and their scholastic success is rather difficult to demonstrate empirically, except perhaps in extreme cases. Indeed, such evidence as does exist points to an absence of a direct link between the way students view their school life and their relative mastery of academic objectives. Because this evidence contradicts our common sense expectations it deserves special attention.

In several of the studies already discussed an effort was made to examine the relationship between student responses to attitude questionnaires and measures of academic success. The results, without exception, were disappointing. Time and again the statistical manipulations of the data reveal the disquieting fact of no significant relationship. The correlation coefficients in Table 11, which are based on responses from the sixth graders that have been discussed, are typical of what has been found.

The main message contained in Table 11 is simply that none of the thirty-two correlation coefficients differs significantly from zero. But there is more to it than that. It is also important to note that the same results were obtained with teachers' grades as with achievement tests. Moreover, similar findings occurred when using either of two student attitude questionnaires.[36] No matter how it is looked at, the relationship is nil between these sixth graders' attitudes toward school and measures of their academic prowess.

Another set of correlations from a study that has already been discussed is presented in Table 12.[37] In this study the students were high school juniors and the attitude measure used was the *Student Opinion Poll*. The achievement information from these students deals only with performance in English, but the inclusion of IQ data affords a rather good indication of what might have been found had achievement scores and grades in other school subjects been available.

Again, the message contained in the correlation coefficients is simple: no apparent relationship exists between student attitudes and academic performance. Also, the relationship is again the same for boys and girls and does not depend on whether achievement test scores or course grades are used in the computations.

One possible explanation of the zero correlations would be that they were caused by the presence of a large group of students who do not feel strongly, one way or the other, about their school

---

[36] The *Student Opinion Poll* has already been described (see pp. 55–56). The *Michigan Student Questionnaire* contains 60 items which focus almost exclusively on the student's opinion of his present teacher (for example, "This teacher makes it fun to study things." "This teacher praises us for good work.") The revised version contains 23 fewer items than does the original. For a fuller description of the instrument and its use in research see Ned A. Flanders, "Teacher influence, pupil attitudes and achievement," OE-25040, Cooperative Research Monograph No. 12 (Washington: U.S. Government Printing Office, 1965).

[37] Diedrich.

Table 11 *Correlations between Sixth Graders' Attitudes toward School and Measures of Their Scholastic Achievement*

ATTITUDE MEASURE	SEX	N	TEACHERS' GRADES				ACHIEVEMENT TESTS			
			Reading	Language Arts	Arithmetic	Science	Reading	Language Arts	Arithmetic	IQ
Student Opinion Poll	Boys	148	.15	.13	.08	.15	.14	.11	.13	.06
	Girls	144	.16	.16	.14	.19	.08	.14	.12	.14
Michigan Student Attitude Inventory (revised)	Boys	148	.01	.01	.00	.06	.08	.02	.06	−.08
	Girls	144	.06	.01	.00	.04	−.07	−.06	−.05	.01

Table 12 *Correlations between High School Juniors'*
Attitudes toward School and Measures
of Their Academic Ability

SEX	N	VERBAL IQ	NONVERBAL IQ	ACHIEVEMENT TEST IN ENGLISH	GRADE IN ENGLISH
Boys	127	.06	.01	.05	.05
Girls	131	−.06	−.07	.05	.10

experience. This possibility was investigated by eliminating students with middling scores on the attitude instrument and by examining the achievement records of students whose scores on the opinionnaire were relatively extreme. When the scholastic performance of students whose SOP scores were at least one and a half standard deviations above the mean was compared with that of students whose SOP scores were correspondingly low, no significant differences appeared. Exactly the same results were obtained in an earlier study employing the same methods.[38]

Although the three studies that have just been discussed all report the same result, the importance of the apparent lack of a relationship requires us to seek evidence elsewhere before a conclusion is reached. Also, most of the evidence to this point has involved the use of the *Student Opinion Poll* and has been obtained from students within a rather narrow geographical region. If similar findings were obtained using students in other parts of the country and with different attitude questionnaires, our confidence in the independence of success and satisfaction in school would be increased.

The study by Tenenbaum previously discussed helps to extend the evidence. Tenenbaum, it will be recalled, constructed a school attitude questionnaire which he administered to 639 sixth and seventh graders in three schools in New York City. The correlation coefficients between those students' responses to the questionnaire and such academic variables as IQ, educational quotient (EQ), proficiency marks, and grade progress ranged from .003 to .13.[39] Again, no relationship between attitudes toward school and academic success.

There is an additional point to be made using Tenenbaum's findings. One of his variables, educational quotient, provides a measure of the extent to which the student is academically advanced or retarded in relation to his ability level. The fact that this variable, like the others, was not found to be correlated significantly with

---

[38] Jackson and Getzels.
[39] Tenenbaum, "Attitudes of elementary school children to school, teachers, and classmates."

attitudes toward school would seem to indicate that even when the effects of differences in ability are sharply reduced the more successful students do not think any better of their school than do the less successful ones.

In another study, this one conducted in Indiana, the investigators developed a diagnostic teacher-rating scale which they administered to 1357 students in grades four through eight.[40] Although they report highly significant differences among individual teachers— for example, some teachers are liked much more than are others— the correlations between expressed attitudes and achievement are about the same as those already reported ($r = .1$ with both achievement and IQ obtained from sub-samples of 527 and 552 students).

A different approach to the problem is reported in a study conducted by L. F. Malpass in a small town in New York.[41] In this investigation 92 eighth grade students responded to two types of projective devices (a sentence completion test and "TAT-type" pictures) designed to reveal their attitudes toward school. The same students also wrote essays about their classroom experiences. A composite rating reflecting his overall view of school life was obtained from each student. The correlation between these composite scores and achievement test performance did not differ significantly from zero. Significant correlations (ranging between .31 and .57) were found, however, between the global estimates of the student's opinions and the grades they received in school. Malpass does not speculate on why the correlations should be found with course grades but not with achievement test scores.

In combination the six studies reviewed thus far provided a rather impressive array of evidence. They involve more than 3000 students from at least 15 schools in several geographical areas. At least five different instruments were used to collect the information concerning student attitudes and a variety of tests were used to obtain the achievement data. Moreover, the six studies cover a time span of 25 years. With the exception of one set of significant correlations with grades the story told by these six investigations is of a piece. Each casts doubt on the common-sense expectation that there will be a noticeable relationship between the way a student feels about his school experience and his relative success in coping with the academic demands of school.

A study recently conducted in Minnesota deserves special men-

[40] Sister M. Amatora Tschechtelin, Sister M. John Frances Hipskind, and H. H. Remmers, "Measuring the attitudes of elementary school children toward their teachers," *Journal of Educational Psychology*, 31:195–203, March 1940.

[41] L. F. Malpass, "Some relationships between students' perceptions of school and their achievement," *Journal of Educational Psychology*, 44:475–482, December 1953.

tion because it contains findings that are contradictory, in certain respects, to those summarized in the last paragraph.[42] In this study the investigator administered the *Student Opinion Poll* to 505 high school juniors and selected extreme scorers who were designated as "highly satisfied" and "highly dissatisfied" students. These groups were compared on the basis of their performance on nine subtests of the *Iowa Test of Educational Development*. The results indicate that the satisfied and dissatisfied students differed significantly (at the .05 level) on seven of the nine scores, with the satisfied group attaining the higher achievement levels. However, when the groups are divided by sex an examination of the mean scores reveals that all of the significant differences were due to the unusually low performance of the small group ($N = 18$) of dissatisfied girls. The investigator offers no explanation of the unusual performance of this group of girls, and because similar results have not been obtained by any other researcher, to the writer's knowledge, it seems proper merely to note this anomaly before moving on to a consideration of the general meaning of the phenomenon in question.

Any evidence that runs counter to common-sense expectations is best approached with healthy skepticism, if not actual disbelief. It is troublesome to change our characteristic views of the world and before we set about trying to do so we want to be sure the effort is necessary. This means, with respect to the topic at hand, that we should consider first the arguments that might be used to discredit the evidence that has been presented.

The most logical target of the skeptic would be the questionnaires used to assess the student's attitudes. He doubtlessly would begin with some form of the general question: How reliable and how valid is the information provided by these paper-and-pencil tests? It is well to remember as we approach this question that we are talking about the merits of several data-gathering procedures rather than a single questionnaire.

Information is not available on all the instruments whose results have been described, but such as there is indicates that these devices would compare favorably with other kinds of questionnaires. The *Student Opinion Poll*, for example, yielded a reliability coefficient (internal consistency) of .85 when tested on a group of about 300 sixth graders. Tenenbaum obtained an equally high reliability coefficient with his questionnaire, as did Sister M. Amatora and her associates with the instrument they developed. Comparable figures are not available for the *Michigan Student Attitude Inventory* or for the procedures employed in the study by Malpass.

Unfortunately, nothing is known about the stability of students'

---

[42] Thomas A. Brodie, Jr., "Attitude toward school and academic achievement," *Personnel and Guidance Journal*, 43:375–378, December 1964.

attitudes over time, but there seems to be no special reason why feelings toward school and teachers would be any less stable than would attitudes toward other aspects of the students' world. They might be expected to change with time, but it is doubtful that they would do so capriciously. The fact that the teachers can predict the scores of students a few days in advance of the administration of the questionnaire provides at least indirect evidence of the stability of the attitudes being examined.

The truthfulness of the students' responses might also be questioned, but again, the greater-than-chance accuracy of the teachers' estimates and the fact that predictable relationship did appear between the expressions of attitudes and other variables (sex, psychological health measures) reduces the power of this explanation. Also, in most of the studies the usual precautions were taken—the assurance of anonymity, no teacher present—to encourage honesty in responding. It is probable that some students did try to cloak their true feelings, but it is doubtful that dishonesty was sufficiently widespread to mask a stable link between attitudes and achievement, if such a link did exist.

Finally, some critics might argue that there are aspects of student attitudes related to differences in achievement but these aspects were not included, or at least were not adequately represented in any of the attitude questionnaires. If this criticism is to be taken seriously, however, the critic must be able to identify the components of attitude that have been overlooked. And this is not easy to do. It is not enough to say that the results might have been different if the research instruments had been different. So far as can be seen the school attitude questionnaires do not have any obvious omissions that would easily explain the results that have been described.

The evidence with respect to the stability and validity of the instruments and the honesty of the students' reports is clearly not sufficient to rule out completely any of the arguments that have been presented thus far. There are, further, the slight but undeniable contradictions to be found in two of the studies. Nonetheless, even with these weaknesses it is safe to conclude that the relationship between attitudes and scholastic achievement, if it exists at all, is not nearly as easy to demonstrate as common sense would lead us to believe it might be. Even though we might want to reserve our final judgment until future studies have been made, the available evidence is sufficient to provoke speculation. Let us assume for the moment that there is little or no relation between the students' attitude toward school and their relative academic success. Why might this be so? And what meaning might this lack of a relationship have for the classroom teacher?

It was acknowledged at the beginning of the last section that certain crude relationships between attitudes and achievement do exist and are visible to most teachers. For example, potential drop-outs probably like school less than do average students and their dislike is coupled with lower-than-average achievement records. Most teachers would take this fact to be incontrovertible. Indeed, it is extreme cases, such as the potential drop-out, or the obviously contented valedictorian at the other extreme, that lead to the general expectation that there will be a linkage between attitude and achievement all along the line.

But suppose the gradations of differences revealed by attitude questionnaires do not represent significant differences in the subjective feelings of the students. Suppose, that is, that a small number of students dislike school intensely and an equally small number are correspondingly positive in their opinion, but that most students have either mixed or very neutral feelings about their classroom experience. Perhaps for attitudes to interact with achievement they have to be extreme, and extreme attitudes, either positive or negative, may be much rarer than is commonly thought.

Involvement and Withdrawal in the Classroom 3

Even when the teacher acts like a broadcasting station, it is doubtful that all the pupils are tuned in. A more plausible model is that the teacher is communicating with different individuals for brief sporadic periods and that these pupils are responding to other stimuli the rest of the time.

Harry F. Silberman, *Journal of Teacher Education,* 14: 235, 1963

Formal social gatherings often begin with a roll call. This official identification of persons present has both ceremonial and practical significance. As ceremony, it enhances the importance of the meeting and helps to create a sense of unity by making each member aware of his fellow participants. More practically, the function of the roll call is to identify absentees.

In schools and other institutions having compulsory attendance the practical value of taking roll outweighs its ceremonial importance. Nothing is more obvious than that a student must be in attendance if he is to enjoy the benefits of instruction, and from a recognition of this truism have sprung teachers' registers, "cut" systems, the job of truant officer, doctor's excuses, and other well-known school practices, all designed to monitor the student's physical presence. Clearly, it makes no sense to begin teaching in an empty classroom.

But the face-to-face confrontation of students and teachers, though necessary, is obviously not enough to ensure the attainment of educational goals. In addition to merely being there the participants must attend in a more profound fashion. They must look at and listen to the objects of their lessons. They must selectively perceive the world of the classroom, shutting out some sources of stimulation and concentrating on others. They must obey commands that tell them to pay attention, to keep working, and to keep their wits about them. In short, they must become involved in their school work.

In education courses and in the professional literature involvement and its opposite, some form of detachment, are largely ignored. Yet, from a logical point of view, few topics would seem to have greater relevance for the teacher's work. Certainly no educational goals are more immediate than those that concern the establishment and maintenance of the student's absorption in the task at hand. Almost all other objectives are dependent for their accomplishment upon the attainment of this basic condition. Yet this fact seems to have been more appreciated in the past than it is today. Henry C. Morrison, for example, had this to say about the subject several decades ago in his widely read text on teaching in high schools:[1]

---

[1] Henry C. Morrison, *The Practice of Teaching in the Secondary School* (Chicago: University of Chicago Press, 1927).

In a sense, the fundamental problem of teaching is to so train the pupil, so arrange his studies and so apply an effective operative technique that he will eventually be able to become so absorbed in any study which in itself is worthwhile. [p. 135]

The development in the pupil of the capacity for willing sustained application, founded only on the expectation that the subject matter will ultimately yield a sustaining interest, is therefore the foundation of any systematic technique of teaching and learning. [p. 106]

Although there are limits to the pedagogical importance of "sustained application," as Morrison himself clearly understood, much can be gained by taking a closer look than is currently fashionable at the occurrence of attention and inattention in the classroom. Indeed, a detailed examination of these seemingly mundane matters provides a vantage point from which to view several enduring educational issues. Such is the purpose of considering them in this chapter.

The material to follow is divided into two parts. Part I deals with the scope of the problem. The central concern in that section is with the extent to which students are in or out of focus, so to speak, while sitting at their desks. Particular emphasis is placed upon the history of research aimed at learning more about this phenomenon. Part II focuses on the teacher's methods of coping with the threat and the reality of student inattention. In that section a special effort is made to relate the teacher's strategies to broader educational concerns.

I

Anyone who has ever taught cannot help having wondered from time to time whether his students were with him or not. Sometimes, of course, it is easy to tell. The student asleep in the back of the room leaves little doubt of his detachment from the on-going activity. Similarly, the student who is frantically waving his hand and has risen half out of his seat in his eagerness to be called on by the teacher looks to be about as involved as he can get. If only the class were neatly divided into the sleepers and the hand-wavers the teacher would have little difficulty in determining the extent of student involvement.

But usually the situation is not that simple. Most of the time students are neither asleep nor half out of their seats in their eagerness to participate. As a result, the teacher must learn to interpret behavioral signs that are considerably more ambiguous. Think of the sights that confront the teacher. Consider, as an instance, the student who sits there with a glassy stare. What thoughts, if any, are running through his head? Are they relevant to the task at hand? What about the girl who is furiously writing over by the window? Are those notes she is taking, or is she dashing off a message to her boyfriend in the back of the room? And what should we think of the young man who is gazing at the ceiling? Is he mentally groping for the insight that will synthesize the hour's discussion, or is he merely conjuring up images to fit the contours of the cracks in the plaster? As every teacher knows, it is sometimes difficult to tell.

As if ambiguity were not enough, the teacher seeking to estimate the extent of involvement in his class is vexed by an additional property of student behavior: its changeableness. Involvement and detachment are not permanent conditions. Rather, they are fleeting psychological states that can, and often do, come and go in the twinkling of an eye. The boy with the glassy stare is now the one who is raising his hand. The girl who was writing furiously a few seconds ago has turned to looking out the window. And the ceiling-gazer has now brought his eyes to rest on the teacher himself. And so it goes. The kaleidoscope of student postures is in constant flux. As every pedagogical novice soon discovers, the classroom world can change abruptly, often in less time than it takes a teacher to turn his head.

The ambiguity and instability of student behavior are sufficiently challenging to consume all the teacher's energies, if he had them to give. But obviously the teacher has other things to do besides trying to figure out whether each and every student is involved in his work. He soon finds, if he tries to undertake the task, that it is practically impossible to keep visual tabs on all the students and to teach at the same time. Although some teachers are clearly more observant than others, even the best of them must find it difficult to exercise a roving eye while engaged in other things. It obviously requires considerable skill to maintain a spirited dialogue with one student while visually scanning the rest of the class. Thus, to the extent that the teacher himself is deeply engrossed in the lesson he likely is blind to many of the events going on around him. At best, therefore, he can only be partially aware of the degree to which his students are involved in legitimate activities. His impression of this involvement, though of great pedagogical significance, cannot be treated as an accurate assessment.

One solution to the problem of assessing involvement would be to bring in an outside observer whose job it would be to describe, as accurately as possible, variations in student attention. Naturally, such an observer would still have to cope with the ambiguity and instability of student behavior. Furthermore, his physical presence would provide an added feature, which might itself affect the amount of involvement in the classroom. (Anyone who has observed for a brief period in a classroom cannot have failed to notice that he too was being observed.) But at least the observer does not have to teach and watch at the same time. Therefore his report might be a little more accurate than that of someone who has to sneak a look, as it were, while doing other things.

Thus, despite obvious difficulties the use of an outside observer has much to recommend it. Not surprisingly, therefore, several investigators have tried this method of gathering information about student attention. Although the direct observation of student attention is engaged in less frequently today than it was thirty or forty years ago, a review of what was learned during the peak of its popularity is illuminating not only for what it can tell us about the phenomenon of attention in the classroom but also for the light it sheds on some of the vagaries of educational research.

Henry C. Morrison, while a Professor of Education at the University of Chicago, was by far the most influential advocate of obtaining measures of students' attention. In *The Practice of Teaching in the Secondary School,* Morrison divided the teacher's task into three sets of interrelated activities or *techniques* to which he applied the identifying labels: *control, operative,* and *administrative.* The first of these, *control techniques,* had to do principally with the establishment and maintainence of group attention and was, in Morrison's view, "the foundation of any systematic technique of teaching."[2] In elaborating on this view he pointed out,

> There is good correlation between the teacher's control technique and his gross effectiveness as a classroom technician. It is fair to assume that the teaching in a large school or in a city school system which is associated with consistently low or erratic attention scores is less effective than is the teaching in another system or school which is associated with consistently high attention scores.[3]

Therefore, Morrison argued, it behooved supervisors and teachers themselves to be as precise as possible in gathering information about this important aspect of classroom life.

The recommended procedures for describing and quantifying students' attention were attractively simple. If a measure of group

---

[2] Morrison, p. 103.
[3] Morrison, p. 128.

attention[4] was desired the observer would seat himself in a corner of the room where the faces of the students were visible and, once a minute, he would visually scan each row, taking a count of the number of students who were obviously inattentive. This number was recorded on a sheet of paper and at the end of the observation period the percentage of student attention was computed by summing the number of students attentive at each minute and dividing that sum by the product of the number of students in the class multiplied by the number of minutes of observation. Usually a more refined measurement was also obtained by calculating the percentage of attentive students during each one-minute interval.

Morrison realized that not all students could be clearly classified as attentive or inattentive but he believed that the number of ambiguous cases would not be great and would decrease as the observer gained experience. He also realized that the presence of the observer might itself be disruptive, thus yielding a false picture of group attention. Because of this danger, he pointed out, the observer occasionally may have to visit the room several times before the pupils become accustomed to his presence, but more often, he predicted, "the observer will need only to wait until the pupils' first curiosity has been satisfied and their minds have resumed normal activity."[5]

At times the teacher himself may wish to observe the behavior of an individual student and make a record of the student's minute-by-minute application to the task at hand. This record would then be shown to the student and its meaning explained. In Morrison's experience such a procedure was often sufficient to bring about a marked improvement in the student's work habits.

According to Morrison, the major reason for measuring group attention was to provide the teacher with information that might help him improve his practice. Although good teachers were expected to command a greater amount of student attention than were poor teachers, the attention scores were not intended to be used by the supervisor to rate his teachers. Rather, they were to serve as diagnostic devices, more advisory than evaluative.

Because Morrison was chiefly concerned with the improvement of teaching, he did not bother to compile descriptive statistics that might give some idea of how much inattention he found to be typical in most classrooms. The goal of the good teacher, in Morrison's judgment, was 100 percent attention. Anything short of that

---

[4] Morrison differentiated between what he called "sustained attention" and "sustained application." Attention referred to situations in which students were watching the teacher or had some other common perceptual focus. Application referred to student attention during individual seatwork.

[5] Morrison, p. 116.

goal was cause for concern, if not alarm. Periods of massive inattention are occasionally revealed as are periods of perfect attention, but the frequency and duration of these extreme conditions cannot be estimated from the information he provides. Fortunately, crude estimates can be indirectly obtained from the work of other investigators, as we shall see.

Even before Morrison's book appeared a few investigators were beginning to examine the educational significance of student attention. One of the most intriguing of these studies was done by William French, one of Morrison's own students, and was submitted, in 1924, as a master's degree in the Department of Education at the University of Chicago.[6] French observed student's behavior during recitation periods conducted by 26 teachers in Drumright, Oklahoma. Twelve of the teachers were on the staff of a junior high school, the remainder were teaching in the fourth, fifth, or sixth grade. The major goal of the study was to compare the observed behavior of both teachers and students with a composite rating of the teacher's ability made by the school principal, by a supervisory test specialist, and by French himself.

The most impressive statistic in French's study was a correlation coefficient of .82, which expressed the relationship between the composite rating of teaching ability and the measures of group attention during recitation periods. Here, then, was evidence in support of Morrison's claims about the pedagogical significance of the teacher's control techniques. With surprising consistency the teachers with the most attentive classes were also the ones most highly regarded by their administrative superiors and, conversely, those with the largest number of inattentive students were placed near the bottom of the group in ratings of teaching ability. The pedagogical moral to be derived from this finding was direct and simple: the able teacher commands his students' attention.

In addition to examining the gross relationship between attention and teaching ability, French reports several findings that help to provide a better picture of attention in the classroom. He points out, for example, that attention scores were slightly higher in the upper grades than in the lower ones. The median percentage of attention was 94 for the junior high school teachers and 91 for the grade school teachers. Projecting this difference to grades above and below those he observed, French conjectured that attention scores might be too high in the final years of high school and too low in the primary grades to serve as indicators of teaching efficiency. He concluded that measures of attention provided the most useful

[6] William C. French, "The correlation between teaching ability and thirteen measurable classroom activities," Unpublished master's thesis, University of Chicago, 1924.

information when applied to "the great middle class of teachers" (the upper grades and the lower high school groups) whose classes generally range in attention from 88 to 95 percent.

Although French's findings must be interpreted cautiously, they are indeed provocative and provide support for the emphasis placed on group attention in Morrison's view of teaching. Of particular note is the fact that differences in group attention from one classroom to another seem to be fairly reliable even though the absolute size of the difference is small. For example, French reports that, "For the seven teachers ranking highest only 6 (recitation) periods of a total of 105 were below .90 (in group attention scores); while for the seven teachers ranking lowest only 19 of the 105 were above .90."[7] Further, he states, "In no recitation did the poorest teacher hold the attention of her class as well as the best teacher did in her poorest recitation."[8] Thus, at least for these teachers, relatively small variations in the percentage of attentive students seemed to make a difference in the measures of teaching effectiveness. Unfortunately, the certainty of this finding is weakened by the fact that French himself was among the persons who rated the teachers. Nonetheless, his study leaves the reader with the urge to learn more about the distributions and meaning of attention scores.

Another early study of student attention focused on the effect of class size on the proportion of attentive students.[9] The plan of the study was to observe what happened in two elementary school classrooms as the number of students in each room was systematically increased, by adding five newcomers each week. The investigator reports that the differences in attention scores between the two classrooms were greater than were the differences between small and large classes. One of the teachers had an average of 90 percent of her students attentive; the average for the other teacher was 81 percent. Moreover, when the first teacher had 50 pupils, group attention was just as high as when there were 23 pupils. These findings are more suggestive than informative, based as they are on the situation in only two classrooms. Nonetheless, they do add at least a scrap of support to the general impression created by Morrison's examples and French's report. Here too it was found that attention scores, on the whole, were rather high and it was suggested that slight differences from one classroom to another might have evaluative significance.

A somewhat different approach to the problem of student attention was taken by Percival Symonds who, in 1925, observed 10

---

[7] French, p. 25.
[8] French, p. 25.
[9] L. Bjarnason, "Relation of class size to control of attention," *Elementary School Journal*, 26:36–41, September 1925.

ninth grade boys (5 who "studied well" and 5 who "studied poorly") during 30 hours of classroom instruction.[10] Symonds' report does not include any mention of the exact amount of time each student was observed to be attentive, although he does say that the students who studied well did not seem better able to concentrate than did those who studied poorly. However, he did find that the studious group showed superiority in the ability to shift their attention from one thing to another. Indeed, this was the most outstanding of all the differences between the two groups. Again, as in the other studies of the same period, an aspect of student attention was reported to be of pedagogical significance.

Within a few years after the publication of Morrison's book several investigators had incorporated his group attention scores into their research plans and some had begun to turn their attention to the technical problems associated with Morrison's technique. C. E. Blume, for example, sought information about the reliability of attention scores.[11] He sent pairs of observers into 17 eighth grade classes and compared the percentages of attention each member of the pair reported. The agreement among observers was rather high, but, again, the variability in attention among the 17 classes was quite small. The range of attention scores was from 90 percent to 98 percent. Blume is careful to warn against using attention scores as a rating device, but in a final section of his report he argues, "That method, other things being equal, that results in high attention is superior to the one that secures indifferent attention."[12]

In the same yearbook in which Blume's report appeared, William S. Gray, then one of Morrison's colleagues, recommended the use of attention scores in the supervision of teachers.[13] Arguing for the advantages of this procedure, Gray states, "Since only a small number, as a rule, are not attending at a given moment, the recording of the essential facts requires very little time."[14] Thus, indirectly, Gray confirms what others have reported: most of the time most of the students are attending to what is going on. Encouraged by a similar finding, one superintendent of schools, after observing

---

[10] P. M. Symonds, "Study habits of high school pupils as shown by close observation of contrasted groups," *Teachers College Record,* 27:713–24, April 1926.

[11] C. E. Blume, "Techniques in the measuring of pupil attention," in *The National Conference of Supervisors and Directors of Instruction, Second Yearbook* (New York: Bureau of Publications, Teachers College, Columbia University, 1929), pp. 37–51.

[12] Blume, p. 51.

[13] W. S. Gray, "Objective techniques in supervising instruction in reading," in *National Conference on Supervisors and Directors of Instruction Second Yearbook* (New York: Bureau of Publications, Teachers College, Columbia University, 1929), pp. 181–192.

[14] Gray, p. 189.

arithmetic classes in his school system, announced, "it is not difficult, by the use of intelligent planning, to secure practically one hundred per cent of pupil attention."[15]

The early enthusiasm over measures of group attention was not shared by all. A. S. Barr, for example, in his pioneering study of good and poor teachers discarded attention scores from his battery of objective measures, explaining in a footnote that the attention records proved too unreliable to be used.[16] Another investigator working under the direction of Carleton Washburne, followed Morrison's procedure in a study designed to compare the individualized study program at the Winnetka schools with a more traditional program in a neighboring elementary school.[17] Rather surprisingly, the percents of attention, when averaged for all visits to each school, were 90 for the Winnetka students and 97.5 for the students in the traditional school. Washburne comments, "[the results] show a small but remarkably consistent tendency of children working under the class method to be more uniformly at attention than those working under the individual method. Of course the question arises whether the fact that a child's eyes are on the teacher or his book indicates that he is really paying attention."[18] Thus, some early doubts were cast on the validity of the attention measures.

Of course Morrison himself realized that attention may be faked, but he felt that this was not a serious problem under normal conditions. Others who applied Morrison's technique took a similar position. C. W. Knudsen, for example, pointed out that the accuracy of attention scores was not their main virtue, and went on to add, "As a matter of fact, pupils often have a way of paying attention when a supervisor is present that is not at all characteristic when the supervisor is absent."[19] Despite his recognition of this inaccuracy, Knudsen continued to advocate the use of group attention scores in the supervision of teaching.[20] Although he does not state his reasons, it seems likely that he believed the amount of faking to be slight and to be relatively constant from one classroom to another.

---

[15] W. E. Long, "Pupil attention in arithmetic," *University of Pittsburgh School of Education Journal*, 3:27–29, 32–33, November–December 1927, p. 33.

[16] A. S. Barr, *Characteristic differences in the teaching performance of good and poor teachers of the social studies* (Bloomington, Ill. Public School Publishing Company, 1929), p. 23.

[17] C. Washburne, Mabel Vogel, and W. S. Gray, "Results of practical experiments in fitting schools to individuals," *Supplementary Educational Monograph, Journal of Educational Research* (Bloomington, Ill. Public School Publishing Company, 1926).

[18] Washburne, Vogel, and Gray, pp. 106–107.

[19] C. W. Knudsen, "A program of high-school supervision," *Peabody Journal of Education*, 7:323–332, May 1930, pp. 326–327.

[20] C. W. Knudsen, *Evaluation and Improvement of Teaching* (New York: Doubleday, 1932).

Knudsen's discussion of the supervisory value of attention scores also contains some hint of the level to which attention must drop before it would be considered unusually low. Apparently if 80 percent or less of the students were attentive the teacher should be considered to have low group control. Thus, once again, there is the implication that most of the time most of the students will be observed to be attentive. An undisclosed number may really have their minds on other matters, but hopefully that number will be small, and since there is no easy way to separate the fraudulent from the genuinely attentive there seems to be no alternative but to ignore the distinction.

The transient quality of student attention is implicitly recognized in Morrison's directions for obtaining group attention scores. He recommended, the reader will recall, that the observer estimate the class' state of attention once a minute. This procedure, if followed, would leave the observer little time for doing anything else during his visit, thus it seems only natural that someone would try to discover whether less frequent observations would yield equally reliable information. The two investigators who sought to answer this question observed 78 classes in junior and senior high school.[21] They followed the standard procedure of assessing group attention once a minute, and then combined the scores obtained at one-, three-, and five-minute intervals. In sum, they found that scores obtained three minutes apart closely resembled those obtained at one-minute intervals, but that a five-minute gap between assessments yielded findings that were markedly different from those obtained with the traditional method. Accordingly, they recommended that observers record group attention scores no less frequently than once every three minutes.

Included in the Brueckner and Ladenberg report is mention of the average amount of attention observed in the classrooms they visited. The overall average percentage for assessments obtained at all three of the time intervals was slightly greater than 91 percent. This figure is quite consistent with the averages reported by other investigators.

Two other investigations need to be added to those that provide some estimate of the amount of attention to be found in an average classroom. The first was conducted in Ohio where student observers in 12 schools spent 150 hours in more than 200 classes.[22] The out-

---

[21] L. J. Brueckner and A. Ladenberg, "Frequency of checking attention and the reliability of the attention quotient," *School Review,* **40**:370–374, May 1933.

[22] R. W. Edmiston and R. W. Braddock, "Study of the effect of various teaching procedures upon observed group attention in the secondary school," *Journal of Educational Psychology,* **32**:665–672, December 1941.

come of all this observing yielded a mean percentage of attention which varied from 80.6 to 88.2 for different kinds of class activities. Students were found to be most attentive during student reports and demonstrations and least attentive during discussions and laboratory periods. The range in the percentages of attention was from 52 to 100 percent.

The second study was conducted in two junior high schools.[23] In one of these schools the students were grouped on the basis of IQ, in the other there was no ability groupings. The goal of the research was to determine whether there was a difference in the level of attention in these two schools. The findings showed that the high ability groups exhibited somewhat more attention than did the lower ability groups, but not much more. In brief, there were no significant differences between the two schools. Attention in both tended to be high. Most of the median group attention percentages were in the 90s. The lowest was 87 percent.

The most direct attacks on the value of Morrison's group attention score came, somewhat surprisingly, from the investigator whose study has just been described. Professor Shannon, who then was on the staff of the Indiana State Teachers College at Terre Haute, conducted two studies whose findings led him to be critical of Morrison's method.[24, 25] One focused on the relationship between attention scores and traditional measures of teaching effectiveness; the other dealt with the relationship between attention and school achievement.

In the 1936 study Shannon had 14 of his graduate students evaluate the performance of a group of student teachers, using three techniques: "score-card" ratings of teachers' traits, general informal estimates (made only by raters who were experienced teachers), and Morrison's attention scores. One hundred and eleven teachers were visited and evaluated, each by at least two of the three techniques. In essence, Shannon found that the score-card measurement and the informal estimate were in greater agreement with each other than either was with the group attention score. This finding led him to conclude that group attention scores were inferior to the other two measures as indicators of good teaching.

The second study, which concerned attention and achievement, employed an experimental design and involved the participation of 100 students from 2 seventh grade and 2 eighth grade classes. The teachers in these four classes were instructed to read to their

[23] J. R. Shannon, "Homogeneous grouping and pupil attention in junior high schools," *Teachers College Journal,* 12:49–52, January 1941.

[24] J. R. Shannon, "A comparison of three means for measuring efficiency in teaching," *Journal of Educational Research,* 29:501–508, March 1936.

[25] J. R. Shannon, "Measure of the validity of attention scores," *Journal of Educational Research,* 35:623–631, April 1942.

students a ten-minute passage on the subject of parachute jumping. Three observers were stationed in each room and attention scores were obtained at one-minute intervals during the teacher's reading. After the reading an achievement test covering the material contained in the passage was administered. The items in the test were keyed to the material being covered at the exact time the observers were making their ratings of group attention.

The overall correlations between attention scores and achievement test scores were .67 for the boys and .34 for the girls. However, the distribution of the attention scores (as usual, most of the students were attentive) and the unknown reliability of the ten-item achievement test make the correlational measures difficult to interpret. Shannon himself chose to overlook the significance of the correlations and pointed instead to the fact that the inattentive students (9 boys and 28 girls were inattentive part of the time) did as well on the material that was covered while their attention was apparently wandering as they did on the material covered during their attentive moments. This finding led Shannon to conclude, "the evidence is damaging to the validity of attention measurement. This conclusion should have been obvious, but evidently Morrison did not think so."[26]

It is difficult today to determine what Morrison, or anyone else for that matter, thought about Shannon's studies. Apparently Shannon himself was not too sure of their meaning, for his use of attention scores to determine the relative superiority of homogeneous or heterogeneous grouping occurred *after* the first of his studies in which the validity of the same scores was brought into question.

Whatever might have been the climate of opinion at the time, Shannon appears to have had the final word. After his "parachute" study, which was published in 1942, Morrison's attention score and the research it generated seem not to be referred to again in the professional literature. From a historical perspective it is not clear why this happened. Judged on the quality of his criticism Shannon should get little of the credit or the blame for the disappearance of studies of classroom attention. Although his investigations were provocative, they came far from providing a rigorous test of the theoretical and practical usefulness of the attention scores, even when those investigations are judged by the research standards of their time.

More important causes of the decline of interest in the study of classroom attention are likely to be found in some of the subtle and not-so-subtle changes that were overtaking the educational and research scenes prior to and following World War II. In education,

---

[26] Shannon, "Measure of the validity of attention scores," p. 631.

perhaps more so than in other fields, the dominant research interests reflect the climate of opinion that permeates the society at large. During the 1930s and 1940s that climate was changing in several ways that must have had a dampening influence on any interest in classroom attention.

Even the word *attention* was out of keeping with the rising interest in progressive education and democratic teaching practices. The idea of trying to keep students' attention had a slightly authoritarian ring to it. The nation as a whole was caught up in the bitter struggle of demonstrating the superiority of democratic social arrangements over those of a more totalitarian cast. In our schools this struggle took the form of trying to demonstrate that discussions were superior to lectures and that warmth and understanding were more important teacher attributes than were strictness and unbending discipline. Although it seems to have passed unnoticed at the time, there was something strangely prophetic about the report of Carleton Washburne and his colleagues who found the Winnetka students less attentive than were their peers in conventional classrooms. At a time when individualized study, group projects, pupil planning, "buzz" sessions, and moveable desks were coming into fashion, the researcher who maintained an interest in what went on during recitation periods was bound to seem a bit quaint, if not downright old-fashioned.

A second kind of change, not quite so obvious as the movement toward more democratic classroom procedures, was the movement, particularly within psychology, from a static to a dynamic view of human affairs. This shift, which was largely coincident with the emergence of Freudian psychology, was expressed by a changing emphasis of research concerns. The interest of many investigators switched from conscious to unconscious processes, from manifest to latent signs of human disorder, from persona to personality. Metaphorically, the change was described as a movement from surface to depth. In education an interest in students' motives began to replace an earlier interest in classroom manners.

Given these changes in the ideological *geist* it is not surprising to find that when the phenomenon of classroom attention re-enters the research literature after World War II the word *attention* does not appear. Also, no mention is made of the earlier work of Morrison and his contemporaries. Rather than relying on the immediate visual information presented by students, investigators turned to less obvious aspects of student behavior. Rather than asking whether or not Johnny looks alert, the researchers now wanted to know: "What is Johnny really thinking about as he sits in class?" The series of studies to which reference is here being made were undertaken by Benjamin Bloom and two of his graduate students at the University of Chicago.[27, 28, 29] The main goal of the studies was to develop a technique for revealing the thought processes of students as they sat in class. This technique, to which Bloom gave the term *stimulated recall,* consisted of making sound recordings of a class session and playing them back to the students within a period of two days from the actual event. The recordings were stopped at critical points and the students were asked to report the thoughts they had experienced during the original situation. These reports were then classified in several ways, but most important was the question of whether the student reported thoughts that were relevant to the topic being discussed at that moment in class. Obviously, if a student's thoughts were irrelevant to the topic at hand he might be considered inattentive, in a psychological sense, no matter how he might appear to a classroom observer.

The specific purpose of Bloom's original study was to compare the thought processes that seem to occur during lectures with those reported to take place during discussions. His subjects for this purpose were obtained from 29 discussion classes and 3 lectures in the undergraduate college of the University of Chicago. Given the purpose of his investigation and the atypicality of his sample, it is somewhat meaningless to contrast Bloom's findings with those of the previous investigators who worked in public school classrooms counting the number of inattentive students. Nonetheless, because several of the previous investigators raised the question of whether some of the students might be falsifying their attention, Bloom's findings with respect to the amount of covert inattention do have some relevance to the topic at hand.

Sixty-four percent of the thoughts reported by the sample of students attending the lectures were about the idea under consideration or a related idea. The equivalent figure for students in discussion classes was 55 percent.[30] In other words, at the selected points during the teaching sessions at least one-third of the class gave testimony of being psychologically absent. And these figures, it must be remembered, were obtained at a college attended by an

---

[27] B. S. Bloom, "Thought processes in lectures and discussions," *Journal of General Education,* 7:160–169, April 1953.

[28] E. L. Gaier, "The use of stimulated recall in revealing the relationship between selected personality variables and the learning process," Unpublished Ph.D. dissertation, University of Chicago, 1951.

[29] Stella B. Schulz, "A study of relationships between overt verbal behavior in the classroom and conscious mental processes of the students," Unpublished Ph.D. dissertation, University of Chicago, 1951.

[30] Although there appeared to be more relevant thought in lectures than in discussions, Bloom concluded that discussions were pedagogically superior' to lectures. His argument rested on the fact that thoughts during discussions more frequently entailed a high order of intellectual effort than did those occurring during lectures.

unusually gifted group of students and staffed by an exceptionally dedicated cadre of teachers. All difficulties of interpretation and comparison notwithstanding, these findings suggest that the amount of inattention common in most classrooms might indeed be significantly greater than the optimistic reports of Morrison and his contemporaries would lead us to believe. This fact does not invalidate the earlier work—it may still be true that about 90 percent of the students *look* attentive (when an observer is in the room)—and in some ways it might increase their significance. If signs of visible attention are found to correlate with achievement measures *despite* the built-in error of feigned interest, there is the possibility that a more accurate assessment of student involvement would relate even more closely to measures of academic success.

The link between thinking and achievement in the classroom was examined in two recent studies using modifications of Bloom's technique.[31, 32] In the first of these Siegal and his associates found a correlation of .59 (which was raised to .61 when the effects of out-of-class learning were controlled) between a measure of the relevance of a students' thoughts and performance on achievement test items keyed to the material covered at the exact time during which introspective reports were requested. In the second study Kraushopf reports a correlation of .56 between estimates of relevant thinking and a test on the total range of material covered during the lecture. He also reports that there was no significant correlation between estimates of relevant thought during the experimental session and a measure of general ability.

The statistics from these two studies cannot be considered definitive. In particular it must be remembered that the investigators did not simply classify students' thought as relevant or irrelevant to the topic of the lesson. Instead, they tried to establish *degrees* of relevance and the correlation coefficients make use of scores that have been weighted in this fashion. Nonetheless, the results are encouraging. A measure that correlates with aspects of achievement without correlating, at the same time, with a measure of general ability is indeed a rare phenomenon in educational research.

Two recent studies contain signs of a reawakening interest in measures of visible attention, similar to those advocated by Morrison, and in one of these investigations an explicit attempt is made to compare the results obtained by direct observation with those obtained by employing a variant of Bloom's stimulated recall tech-

[31] L. Siegel, Lila C. Siegel, P. J. Capretta, R. L. Jones, and H. Berkowitz, Students' thoughts during class: a criterion for educational research," *Journal of Educational Psychology,* 54:45–51, February 1963.

[32] C. J. Krauskopf, "Use of written responses in the stimulated recall method," *Journal of Educational Psychology,* 54:172–176, June 1963.

nique. This comparison was undertaken by Bryce Hudgins, who sent a pair of observers to collect group attention scores in nine sections of English in a junior high school. Each section was visited five times during a week of data collection. In addition to assessing group attention the observers also interrupted the classes as many as five times during a period in order to administer a self-report questionnaire that asked each student to report on his degree of attention during the time interval immediately preceeding the interruption. The pupils' responses to the questionnaire were classified according to whether they revealed "negative social involvement" or "subject matter relevance." Reports of "relevant" thoughts were assigned weighted scores according to their apparent degree of relevance, which ranged "from tangential and passive thoughts about the subject matter to those that reflect comprehension or higher order cognitive operations."[33] Thus, each self-report yielded two scores, one reflecting the presence or absence of inattention, the other reflecting the quality of attentive thought. Both of these scores were compared with the observers' estimates of group attention and with a similar estimate made by the classroom teacher.

Hudgins reports statistically significant negative correlations, ranging from —.52 to —.70, between observers measures of attention and self-reports of inattention in five of the nine classes. In only two classes, however, were observers' judgments significantly related to the quality of the relevant thoughts reported by the students themselves. In other words, the observers seemed able to detect gross inattention with some accuracy in five of the classrooms, but their front-of-the-room observations were not revealing when compared with more subtle distinctions in the quality of the students' thinking. The teachers' judgments agreed in general with those of the outside observers, but their agreement was less close with the students' self-reports than was that of the outsiders. Though inclusive, these findings do provide some encouragement for the continued use of the group attention measure, while at the same time suggesting that efforts to learn more about the attentiveness of students cannot be limited to the information obtained by such direct procedures.

A second recent study using measures of visible attention was conducted by Henriette M. Lahaderne, who examined attitudinal and scholastic correlates of attention in four sixth-grade classrooms.[34] Miss Lahaderne collected repeated measures of attention

---

[33] Bryce B. Hudgins, "Attending and thinking in the classroom," Symposium paper presented to the American Psychological Association meeting, New York, September 1966, mimeographed (14 pp.), p. 8.

[34] Henriette M. Lahaderne, "Attitudinal and intellectual correlates of attention: a study of four sixth-grade classrooms," A paper read at the meeting of the American Educational Research Association, New York, February 1967.

over a three-month period during which she spent about nine hours in each room. The observational procedure, which was the same as that employed by Hudgins and was similar to that advocated by Morrison, yielded three interrelated measures for each student: the number of times he was judged to be attentive, the number of times he was judged to be inattentive, and the number of times the observer felt himself to be uncertain in his judgment. The design of the study called for these measures to be compared with the students' responses to two questionnaires intended to reveal their attitudes toward school as well as their performance on a group intelligence test and on four standardized achievement tests in reading, arithmetic, and language arts.

There were two major findings. First, there was almost no relation between measures of students' attitudes toward school and measures of their attention in class. The average correlation coefficient describing this relationship was .10. Second, a set of positive correlations was found to express the relationship between the students' attention in class and their performance on intelligence and achievement tests. The size of these correlations ranged from .37 to .53. Moreover, when the effect of differences in intelligence was statistically controlled, the relationship between attention and achievement did not disappear, although the linkage between the two was found to be different from one subject matter area to another. Thus, Miss Lahaderne's findings enhance the general importance of classroom attention as an educationally significant variable. Although the absence of a linkage between the attention scores and students' attitudes poses an interesting problem, the presence of a firm linkage with achievement measures preserves the status of *observable* attention as a legitimate concern in educational affairs.

What, then, are the chief conclusions to be derived from systematic studies of classroom attention, starting from the early work of Morrison and extending to these most recent reports? First, although the amount of attention may vary considerably from class to class and even from minute to minute within a class, it would seem that most of the time most students are attending to the content of the lesson. Second, the amount of attention in the classroom is often less than meets the eye. Researchers were aware of this fact from the beginning and Bloom's study gives some hint of how extensive the faking of attention might be. Third, the amount of attention, even when crudely estimated by an outside observer, seems to be significantly related to other educational variables, such as scores on achievement tests and estimates of teacher effectiveness. There is also the suggestion that the amount of attention may not be closely related to the students' intellectual ability. In sum, these conclusions provide ample justification for further study and speculation.

But even if the results of empirical investigation were not as promising as they are, there are at least two other reasons for pushing forward in our attempt to understand the phenomenon of classroom attention. First, teachers tend to worry about inattentive students, no matter what the statistics might say about the relative achievement of such individuals. As will be shown in the following chapter, an estimate of pupil attention is commonly used by teachers to judge their personal effectiveness in the classroom. The possibility of massive inattention, signalling the loss of the teacher's authority, is frequently reported as a dominant fear among beginning teachers.[35]

Second, students also worry at times about their inability to remain focused on the task at hand. Boredom is one of the chief complaints of students who are having difficulty with school. The inability to concentrate is a recurring sympton in reading clinics and child guidance centers. Indeed, many clinicians see it as a central issue in much of psychopathology. Thus, the fact that most of the students may be attentive most of the time does not reduce the significance of the problem for either teachers or students. The scope of the problem, in other words, is only partially described by counting, by whatever method, the number of daydreamers in the classroom.

II

Although Morrison and his colleagues of a generation ago, correctly ascribed considerable importance to the phenomenon of classroom attention, there is a sense in which they overstated their case. It is now apparent that their insistence on having teachers seek 100 percent attention in their classes was rather naïve. There are several reasons why this is so.

First, as Morrison himself clearly understood (although his critics were to claim he did not), the signs of overt attention are not always trustworthy indicators of the pupil's actual state of mind. As we have seen, all eyes on the teacher does not necessarily mean all thoughts on the topic at hand. The teacher who became exclusively concerned with the visual focus of his pupils was likely to end up achieving only a kind of surface conformity to his demands.

---

[35] See, for example, J. Gabriel, *Emotional Problems of the Teacher in the Classroom* (Melbourne, Australia: F. W. Cheshire, 1957).

Second, as the results of Bloom's stimulated recall technique make clear, important differences exist among those students who are cognitively attentive to what is going on in class. There are, in other words, degrees or, perhaps, kinds of attention. Sometimes students behave like simple recording instruments, listening to what the teacher or their classmates are saying, but not thinking much about it—just "getting the facts," so to speak. At other times, the students may be involved in a much more active intellectual activity bearing on the topic at hand. Some may be relating what they have just heard to previous knowledge, others may be evaluating the general worth and future usefulness of what they have just learned. Indeed, they may become so immersed in these tangential but highly relevant thoughts that they stop listening, for a time, to what is being said. This type of inattention is obviously very different from that which involves thoughts about completely irrelevant matters. The teacher may not mind a certain amount of this "relevant inattention." In fact, he may even encourage it.

Third, the goal of attention for attention's sake is somewhat antithetical to the broader goals of education. The teacher is not merely an entertainer, interested in keeping his audience spellbound. Nor is he merely a shop foreman whose job it is to keep his workers at their task. Rather, he is commited to the more important goal of improving the well-being of the pupils in his charge. He must seek their attention in order to achieve this goal, but attention is only instrumental and, therefore, of secondary importance. If all the teacher sought were the eyes of his students riveted on him or on their workbooks his task would be much simpler than it truly is. He might spend the day telling jokes or cracking the whip if this were all he wanted. But obviously this is not all. The trick is to get the students to pay attention while engaged in activities judged to be of benefit to them. And that, as every teacher knows, is a large order.

The strategies for keeping students engrossed in their work include actions of two very different sorts. One has to do with the maintenance of appropriate working conditions, with the prevention or elimination of extraneous disruptions. The other has to do with the appropriateness of course content, with the "fit," as it were, between the students and the material being studied. The first involves the seemingly trivial business of maintaining order in the classroom. The second involves the seemingly important business of making curricular decisions. But the apparent triviality of the one set of strategies and importance of the other set is often exaggerated in educational discussions. The teacher seeking the attention of his students cannot afford to ignore either one.

The thin tissue of reality that binds the attention of a class during a discussion or that keeps a student focused on his book during a

103

period of individual study may be easily pierced by either internal or external disturbances. A noticeable amount of the teacher's time, at least in the lower grades, is spent in coping with these minor emergencies. A less noticeable, but no less important, portion of his time is spent in establishing rules of conduct that will prevent these disturbances from occurring.

By the time students reach the middle grades the common rules of classroom conduct are so well understood (if not always obeyed) that a slight shake of the teacher's head or a click of his fingers is enough to bring a violator back into line. The ease with which these acts of management are accomplished in the upper grades tends to make the rules themselves seem unimportant. Yet this is only so because the controls are taken for granted by most older students. At the lower grade levels when the rules are being established their relevance to the problem of student attention is much more salient.

The several rules of order that characterize most elementary school classrooms all share a single goal: the prevention of "disturbances." In the lower grades these disturbances may have destructive or aggressive overtones. By the upper grades they are simply annoying or disruptive of on-going activities. Although the specific rules change somewhat from grade to grade and from room to room there is sufficient similarity among them to warrant a discussion of the general forms they take. The rules of order to be found in most classrooms can be grouped into five major classes. These deal with the questions of 1) who may enter and leave the room; 2) how much noise is tolerable; 3) how to preserve privacy in a crowded setting; 4) what to do when work assignments are prematurely finished; and 5) how far to go in establishing the classroom equivalent of social etiquette. Simply because these matters are seldom discussed in any systematic way each is worthy of brief elaboration here.

The question of who may enter and leave the room is of particular importance (as are most of the others) in self-contained classrooms where the students must spend the bulk of their day within the same four walls. The most common reason for individual students requesting to leave the room is, of course, to use the toilet facilities. As a result, almost every elementary classroom has some established routine for accomplishing the orderly entrance and exit of individual students. The problem of entrance and exit does not end, of course, with the establishment of rules for the use of the restrooms. Commonly it is necessary to establish rules concerning the mass arrival and departure of students. These rules include not only the times at which students are expected to arrive and depart, but also the penalties that are to befall latecomers ("Get a pass from the office."), the specific procedures for moving in and out of the room ("Now the girls may get their coats and line up."), and the like. Finally, there are often rules that control the unexpected entrance of visitors into the classroom ("Visitors must sign in at the principal's office."). It is hardly necessary to point out that the regulations governing the entrance and exists of students are not only intended to prevent disruptions within the teacher's own class, but also within the other classes in the building. Also, the rules are often designed as much to prevent particular students from escaping their duties as to preserve the peace and calm of the class session.

Classrooms, by and large, are relatively quiet places and it is part of the teacher's job to keep them that way. Again, the procedures by which the teacher accomplishes this goal vary from grade to grade and from classroom to classroom; also, there are surely differences in the absolute level of noise particular teachers are willing to endure. Despite these differences it is likely that every elementary teacher has to cope, from time to time, with the problem of excessive noise. Frequently teachers of very young students establish routine procedures for signaling that the tolerable limits of noise have been exceeded (they may turn the lights off or play a chord on the piano to signal quiet). Such signals are typically followed by brief exhortations on the necessity of less noise. In the middle and upper grades it is quite common for the teacher to look up from what he is doing and say something like, "Voices, class." By the time students reach those grade levels no further explanation is needed.[36]

A common problem in elementary classrooms is how to prevent students from disturbing each other during periods of individual seatwork and study. The solution has to do partly with maintaining a relatively low noise level, but it usually entails more than that. Students sometimes move quietly about the room on seemingly legitimate errands (going to the pencil sharpener) in the course of which they pause to interrupt one of their classmates who is engrossed in his work. Under these circumstances it is customary for the teacher to question the legitimacy of the student's activity ("Johnny, why are you out of your seat?") and insist that he return to his own work.

When students are expected to work on assignments in class it is inevitable that some will finish before the others. This common situation gives rise to many of the disturbances with which the elementary teacher must deal. The student with "nothing to do" is

---

[36] In this connection it is worth noting that the authors of the *Stanford-Binet Intelligence Test* expect the average ten-year-old to give two reasons why children should not be too noisy in school. Thus, by the time he is in the fourth grade the average youngster is expected not only to know the rule but to understand its logic and to be able to explain it to others.

often the one who creates disruptions for others. Accordingly, many teachers provide activities for students to engage in during the time between assigned tasks. These activities may be nothing more than "busywork" ("Why don't you clean out your desks?") or they may have some intrinsic educational worth ("You may read a library book when you have finished."). But whatever the content of the recommended activity, most elementary school teachers try to remove the potential threat to group attention created by the idle student.

A final set of rules that bears at least tangentially on the problem of maintaining students' attention can be grouped under the general heading of classroom etiquette. These include the polite and thoughtful things to say and do while behaving as a student. They include such things as raising hands in order to be recognized, suppressing the temptation to laugh at or deride a classmate's errors, standing in line without pushing, and the like. As is true for common courtesies in general, violations of these rules are often the occasion for antagonism and, thus, serve to disrupt the smooth flow of social events. Teachers of younger children must often pause to remind their students of their obligations in these matters.

Here, then, is one way of organizing the rules that can be observed to operate in most elementary classrooms. The flow of traffic in and out of the room, the level of noise, the movement of students from one part of the room to another, the behavior of idle students, and breaches of social etiquette, each of these classes of events can serve to destroy the work orientation of the entire group or of individual students. The teacher's techniques for dealing with these events are usually discussed under the general heading of classroom management, a topic that, like attention per se, seems strangely anachronistic as the focus of an educational discussion. Yet it is quite clear that the teacher's success as a teacher depends in no small measure on his ability to deal with these trivial aspects of school. The teacher who has "lost control" of his class, as the expression goes, cannot compensate for that deficiency by doing an especially good job of evaluation or by spending extra time with his remedial reading group. In an educational sense, when group control is lost, all is lost.

Teachers, particularly at the beginning of their careers, realize the importance of these managerial skills and are usually quite concerned about their ability to cope with this aspect of their professional function. When teachers display signs of anger in the classroom—a not uncommon happening, though rarely seen during short-term visits—the events responsible for the display commonly entail some violation of one of the rules that have just been discussed.

Indeed, as educational critics are quick to point out, the maintenance of group control becomes, for some teachers, the core of their professional concern. Sometimes, it would seem, students are made to sit still and be quiet not because their movement and talk will disrupt the attention of the class or the solitary work of their classmates, but because silence itself is believed to have some intrinsic pedagogical value. This view, like that which tolerates too much social chaos, creates an unhappy state of affairs in the classroom. Order, though desireable, is not enough, and when carried to extremes it may no longer even be desireable. Once the teacher has mastered the mundane, though fundamental, business of managing the social traffic in his room he is still confronted with important problems that bear upon students' attention. He must still decide how to ensure a more fundamental kind of attention than that achieved by the command, "All eyes front, please." The crucial problem is what to do once the room has grown quiet and all eyes are on the teacher.

There would seem to be three major strategies for increasing the involvement of students beyond the limits established by techniques of classroom management. One would be to alter the curriculum in such a way as to bring course content closer to the needs and interests of the students. Another would be to group the students in such a way as to create a better "fit" with established course content. A third would be to inject novelty, humor, "human interest," into a lesson, or in some other way to enliven artificially an otherwise dull activity. Fortunately, these three strategies are not mutually exclusive and, therefore, teachers do not have to choose among them. All three can be observed to operate in most classrooms. In some instances they have been initiated by the teachers themselves, in others they are the result of administrative decisions or arise from qualities of the available instructional materials.

The modification of the curriculum to fit the "natural" interests and needs of pupils is, as every educator knows, a cornerstone in the doctrines of progressive education. From a belief in the advisability of such a modification have grown the many innovations (often nothing more than fads) that swept through the schools in the twenties and thirties and that continue to color present practices. The unit plan, the project method, the activity school, pupil planning, and similar methodologies were, and continue to be, the mark of the modern elementary school. The rationale for each of these procedures clearly embraced more than a concern over the problems of pupil's inattention and there is no clear evidence to show that attention per se was enhanced by any of these practices. Nonetheless, there is at least a logical appeal to the belief that students will become more engrossed in activities in which they are naturally interested than activities that have been preselected for them and that bear no relation to their immediate concerns.

The selection of students to fit established curricular activities is also, in a sense, consonant with the doctrines of progressive education. But instead of modifying the curriculum to suit a particular group of students, this procedure calls for assembling groups of students whose abilities or interests are appropriate for particular educational content. The selection may be done by the student himself, as in the elective system common in high schools and colleges, or it may be done for him, as in the various grouping procedures common in the lower grades. Again, elective systems and grouping practices did not spring up in direct response to problems of students' inattention and, also again, there is no concrete evidence that students so selected are any more immersed in school work than those who are not. But, logically at least, they ought to be.

As every student knows, some teachers are lively and others are dull, some class sessions are exciting and others boring. Moreover, the difference often does not seem to reside in the content of the lesson itself or in the material being used but rather in the manner in which the class is conducted. Some teachers seem to be able to make even the dullest subject exciting and others somehow manage to make even the most exciting subject dull. Although the methods for enlivening a class session are too numerous to catalogue (and many are probably known only to the teachers who practice them), the major techniques are sufficiently well known to make even a partial cataloging unnecessary.

It is perhaps also unnecessary to cite evidence showing that devices such as the insertion of novelty or humor into a lesson really "work," that is that they contribute to the amount of student attention, but here some crude empirical evidence is available. In his well-known book on the personality characteristics of teachers David Ryans presents data showing that teachers who were judged (by observers) to be "stimulating" and "creative" tended to have students who were judged (by the same observers) to be "alert" rather than "apathetic."[37] Moreover, of all the teacher characteristics rated by Ryans and his associates "stimulating" and "creative" were the only ones that seemed to have a noticeable and consistent effect on pupil behavior.

This brief discussion of the three most common strategies for

---

[37] D. G. Ryans, *Characteristics of Teachers* (Washington, D.C.: American Council on Education, 1960).

enhancing student attention (details of classroom management aside) should be sufficient to return the topic to the broader perspective from which it was viewed in the beginning of the chapter. The problem, as almost every serious student of the process has clearly recognized, is not just how to maintain an orderly classroom in which students look alert (although the difficulties of that task cannot be easily dismissed), rather it is how to foster a more enduring state of involvement in educational affairs. These two conditions, as Dewey pointed out, are correlative but not synonymous.[38]

The more enduring form of attachment to school work is of the sort that extends beyond the time limits of particular class sessions and even beyond the physical boundaries of the classroom itself. It is connected with those pervasive motivational states that go by such names as interests, attitudes, and values. It becomes anchored, in other words, in the structure that gives shape to the habitual actions of the student.

Involvement in this deeper sense cannot be feigned in the same way as can the surface manifestations of perceptual attention. Students may falsify their appearances but not the underlying conditions that the appearances are intended to convey. They may fool the teacher, in other words, but they cannot as easily fool themselves. For this reason, if for no other, involvement is a more significant educational goal for the teacher to strive toward than is Morrison's ideal of 100 percent attention. In fact, when viewed from this broader perspective involvement begins to look so significant that it is necessary to ask whether it is important for the teacher to worry about anything else.

So long as students are truly involved in some activity does it matter much what the activity is? There are some educators who come close to answering "no" to this question, at least when it refers to the activities of young children. William Heard Kilpatrick, for example, although he placed some strictures on how it might be achieved, ranked the goal of the pupils' commitment, or "wholeheartedness," so high on his scale of educational values that all else seemed relatively unimportant. As he put it:

> This matter of commitment is so important as to demand emphasis. The individual pupil inevitably will learn in the degree that he himself accepts the activity or the enterprise or the experience undertaken. The teacher will accordingly

---

[38] J. Dewey, "The relation of theory to practice in education," *National Society for the Study of Education, Third Yearbook, Part I.* (Bloomington, Ill.: Public School Publishing Company, 1904), pp. 9–30.

work, through the process of group discussion and choice, to get the individual learners and the class as a whole committed as wholeheartedly as possible to the activity chosen.[39]

In Kilpatrick's view the alternative of artificially enlivening otherwise dull material, which we have discussed as one strategy for achieving involvement, was unattractive. He left no doubt of his position on this part.

> Let it be noted, emphatically, that in teaching at its best we do not first choose subject matter, then ask how to make it interesting. . . . The new (view of education) starts where the child is so as to capitalize on the child's personally directed activity springing from his real interest.[40]
> It is what pupils do of themselves that brings the best learning results, both in direct learning and in concomitant learnings. We can thus say, paradoxically, that the teacher's aim is to give as little help as possible, that is, to give the least degree of direct help consistent with the best personal work on the part of the pupils.[41]

In other words, although Kilpatrick advocated that teachers seek the involvement of their students, certain methods of attaining that goal were clearly superior to' other methods. The reasons for their choice are of course closely connected with his views of the good life toward which the process of education contributes. The purpose here is not to analyze Kilpatrick's view critically, but merely to show the centrality of the concept of involvement in the position of one prominent educator.

The trouble with all of these plans for achieving student involvement is that there are limits to the extent to which they can be employed. Moreover, these limits do not necessarily arise, as they did in the case of Kilpatrick's preferences, out of philosophic disagreements over the ends of education. Rather, they spring from some of the givens of the classroom on which we have focused in previous chapters.

The alteration of the curriculum to suit the needs and interests of the students is limited by the harsh fact that most students have to be in school whether they want to be or not. Also, it fails to distinguish between stable and transitory aspects of the students' motivations. Johnny may be interested in learning how to play the recorder, but not always at precisely the time when he is expected to be.

---

[39] W. H. Kilpatrick, *Philosophy of Education* (New York: Macmillan, 1951), p. 306.
[40] Kilpatrick, p. 305.
[41] Kilpatrick, p. 307.

The selection of students to fit a particular curriculum is limited by the population of our schools. The teacher may group his students for certain activities but the fit achieved by this method is approximate at best. Even when the tailoring is more exact, as in the various plans for individualizing instruction, the crowds remain to pull at the student's attention and to divert the teacher's energy. In brief, there are limits to a tutoring model when applied to a group setting.

Even the teacher's efforts to make his class sessions lively and interesting do not represent an unconstrained method for ensuring student involvement. First, novelty, as we all know, "wears off." The method that captivated the students today becomes the same old routine tomorrow. Moreover, the novelty of the class session is nested, as it were, within the larger network of rules, regulations, and routine that colors the working of the school as an institution. Variety may provide the spice of life in the classroom, but it is spice sprinkled on top of a rather bland and unpalatable mixture. Second, even if a teacher is particularly adroit at "hamming it up" or otherwise adding zest to the daily routine, he must continually remind himself that his job is to teach, not merely to entertain. He can seek to involve his students, but his ultimate goal is to benefit them.

What, then, does all of this say about the problem of inattention in the classroom? Four conclusions seem warranted. First, it looks as though inattention, as an educational problem, were here to stay, although the teacher's actions may increase or decrease its severity. Second, attention and involvement are not the same conditions and the teacher would do well to keep the distinction in mind. Even though he might labor to control attention and though he may be forced to rely on signs of alertness as indicators of involvement, it is the latter condition, rather than the former, that he is seeking to cultivate. Third, in the cultivation of human potential, involvement, like love, is not enough. Student interest is important but it is not a sure guide to the value of the educational activity in question. This conclusion implies that the teacher cannot cheat as he goes about seeking the wholehearted engagement of his students. That is, he cannot lay aside his concern for their future development while focusing on their here and now actions. Fourth, and finally, inattention may have its roots not only in the content of the lesson *per se* nor in psychological deficiencies within the student but rather in the nature of the institutional experience called "going to school." Often it is school that is boring, not just arithmetic or social studies. The school experience, in other words, is more than the sum of its parts. Teachers might remember such things as they contemplate the nodding student in the back row.

Teachers' Views 4

Now, in teaching as in several other things, it does not matter much what your philosophy is or is not. It matters more whether you have a philosophy or not. And it matters very much whether you try to live up to your philosophy or not. The only principles of teaching which I thoroughly dislike are those to which people pay only lip service.

George Polya, *Mathematical Discovery*

In teaching, as in every craft, there are masters from whom apprentices can and should learn. Although perfect agreement on who deserves the title may not exist, it is likely that in every school system there could be found at least a handful of teachers who would be called outstanding by almost any standard. The profession as a whole might gain much from such persons, but, as Dewey observed,

> ... the successes of such individuals tend to be born and to die with them; beneficial consequences extend only to those pupils who have personal contact with such gifted teachers. ... the only way by which we can prevent such waste in the future is by methods which enable us to make an analysis of what the gifted teacher does intuitively, so that something accruing from his work can be communicated to others.[1]

Perhaps, as Dewey's suggestion implies, the ideal way to learn from such teachers is to watch them in action. Certainly most of our teacher educators behave as if this were so. Observation typically plays an important part in teacher training programs and it is being used increasingly in educational research. But the teacher's classroom behavior does not always reveal what we want to know. Occupational attitudes, the feelings of satisfaction and of disappointment accompanying success and failure, the reasoning that lies behind action—these and many other aspects of a craft are scarcely visible except through conversations with a person who has experienced them. And it is not only *what* the practitioner says that is revealing. His way of saying it and even the things he leaves unsaid often contain clues to the nature of his experience. Consequently, talk is necessary, particularly talk about the professional aspects of life in the classroom. In this chapter professional shop-talk with 50 outstanding teachers provides the data with which to examine several aspects of the teacher's work.[2]

A major difficulty in following Dewey's advice about analyzing

---

[1] John Dewey, *The Sources of a Science of Education* (New York: Liveright, 1929), pp. 10–11.

[2] In the interests of style and readability, the teachers' dialogues appear in edited form.

what the gifted teacher does is contained in the first step of deciding which teachers shall be considered gifted. The criteria of teaching effectiveness are notoriously elusive. Selection according to one standard, such as growth in student achievement, will not necessarily duplicate the results obtained by applying some other standard, such as the judgment of administrative superiors.[3] Under these circumstances the best approach to the problem might be to apply many different criteria, selecting as gifted only those teachers who are outstanding on all or most of them. Unfortunately, the cost and complexity of such a procedure make it impractical except in research focusing exclusively on the question of teacher effectiveness. If we are to move ahead in answering other questions before the debate over the definition of good teaching is adequately resolved, the only alternative is to select the criterion that seems most appropriate for a particular purpose, and then use proper caution in treating the results.

In gathering the material to be discussed in this chapter the judgments of administrators were used to identify a group of out-standing teachers. It is recognized that administrators may differ in their definitions of good teaching, and their direct knowledge of some teachers' classroom practices must surely be minimal. None-theless, in most school systems, reputations have a way of spreading, and after a time a teacher's merits, as perceived by students, parents, and fellow teachers, and as reflected in test scores and other indica-tors of pupil achievement are likely to become known to the administrator, particularly when the teacher is judged to be un-usually good or bad. Of course when the evidence is scanty or conflicting, the administrator may have to rely on his own contact with a teacher to make a judgment. But, hopefully, for a few fortunate individuals the signs of teaching talent are neither scanty nor conflicting. If the administrator were required to nominate as outstanding only a very small number of his staff presumably he would tend to choose those for whom there is this surfeit of evidence. His nominees—the teachers to whom he points with pride—seem like reasonably attractive objects of study if we hope to learn some-thing about teaching from those who have the reputation of prac-ticing it with great skill.

[3] The interested reader will find several studies of the criterion of effectiveness discussed in: N. L. Gage (ed.), *Handbook of Research on Teaching* (Skokie, Ill.: Rand McNally, 1963); J. W. Getzels and P. W. Jackson, "Research on the variable teacher: some comments," *School Review*, **68:** No. 4, 1961; P. W. Jackson, "The teacher and individual differences," *Sixty-First Yearbook of the National Society for the Study of Education, Part I* (Chicago: University of Chicago Press, 1962), Chapter 5; and W. Rabi-nowitz and R. M. W. Travers, "Problems of defining and assessing teacher effectiveness," *Educational Theory*, 3:212–219, July 1953.

After the teachers have been selected, or at least a method for identifying them agreed upon, the question of what to talk to them about becomes paramount. What is that special "something accruing from his work" to which Dewey referred? And is that something communicable?

Because the general purpose of the interviews was to find out how a group of good teachers viewed life in the classroom, a logical beginning might be to focus on the quality of their teaching efforts. Thus, the opening question becomes, in short, how do they know when they are doing a good job in the classroom? The teachers responded readily to this question and, as will be seen, their answers challenge several of our current educational ideas and practices.

A second set of questions derive from the general theme of the essays in this book. These questions concern the relationship between the teacher's work and the institutional framework in which he and his students are embedded. The principal concern in this portion of the interview was with the teacher's reaction to the use of two forms of authority—his own and that of his administrative superiors. Two questions were particularly effective in uncovering these reactions. One dealt with the ways in which the teacher's personal style of work had changed over the years; the other dealt with the teacher's feelings about having his own work evaluated.

A final set of questions concerned the personal satisfactions that come from being a teacher. These questions were based on the assumption that something besides a monthly paycheck kept these teachers coming back to the classroom year after year. The teacher's replies not only substantiated this assumption but also revealed an aspect of the teacher's world view that might help to make the school experience less painful for young children than it might otherwise be.

Next, a word about the teachers whose views will be discussed. As was noted, our interviewees, with one or two exceptions, were nominated by administrators and supervisors believed to have first-hand knowledge of the quality of the teachers' work. The nominators were requested to select teachers who seemed to be doing outstanding jobs in their schools. Usually no more than one or two interviewees were chosen from each school. Therefore, as perceived by their administrative superiors, these teachers comprise the top 5 or 10 percent of the instructional staff. The sample was drawn chiefly from suburban communities surrounding Chicago. A small number of teachers from a metropolitan private school also participated.

The interviews were tape-recorded and usually were conducted in the teacher's classroom after school. The average interview lasted about 40 minutes; a few ran for more than an hour. The interviewees knew that we wanted to talk to teachers who had earned a highly favorable reputation in their school system. The teachers were assured that their replies would be treated confidentially and that they would not be revealed in a way that might identify the person who made them.

A sample as small and as highly select as the one considered here is hardly representative of teachers in general. Nonetheless, the responses of these 50 teachers were examined in the hope that some generalizations about the teaching process might emerge. Thus, it is necessary to set some crude limits within which such generalizations might operate. To the extent that inference to a larger population is warranted, the present sample is probably best thought of as representing those elementary school teachers who rise to positions of leadership and respect in "advantaged" school systems.

Having acknowledged the restrictions that must be placed on inferential statements it is helpful to take a closer look at the question of what can be said about other teachers on the basis of the responses from the 50 who were interviewed. One way of rephrasing this question is to ask whether or not an overwhelming majority of elementary teachers might answer our questions in much the same way as those we interviewed. Perhaps classroom life is not the same for the run-of-the-mill teacher as for teachers with enviable reputations. The answer to this question is unknown and obviously would require comparing the responses of a group of *average* teachers (almost as difficult to define as *outstanding!*) with those of a group such as the one used in this study.

Yet even without waiting for data from a more representative sample it is safe to predict that some teachers will look like the ones portrayed here and others will not. The question of how many are included in the term *some* would be of great interest if our goal were to produce a demographic description of the entire teaching population. It would also be of interest if our goal were to identify the unique characteristics of the good teacher. But this chapter aims at neither goal. Rather the goal is the more modest one of seeing how some highly admired teachers view life in the classroom and then speculating on the consequences of the views they hold.

An analogy might be helpful here. If a group of lawyers, selected as outstanding by circuit court judges, was found to be critical of the Supreme Court, that fact would be important within certain contexts irrespective of whether or not the same views were held by the general membership of the legal profession. Similarly, if a group of teachers, thought to be unusually talented by their superiors, was found to be uneasy about certain aspects of their work or was found to endorse certain teaching practices enthusiastically, that finding would have significance irrespective of whether or not the same views were shared by others. The importance of what such a group thinks stems from the fact that these are the teachers, presumably, to whom special awards would be given if merit pay or other methods of recognizing talent were instituted within the schools in which they work. These are the people to whom beginning teachers might be directed when they seek professional advice. These are the staff members most likely to have student teachers assigned to their rooms. They are also the ones to whom outside visitors are most frequently introduced. In short, these teachers often serve as models for others. If it turned out that these model teachers resembled the average teacher in important respects it would be difficult to determine whether that resemblance spoke to the effectiveness of the model, or the inability of the judges to discriminate between the average and the exceptional or neither. In any event, judgments such as those just described are being made constantly in schools. The qualities of the persons on whom these professional kudos are bestowed may be expected to have consequences for both theory and practice.

As has been mentioned, the questions in the interview had three foci: the teacher's self-evaluation, the uses of institutional authority, and the satisfactions to be derived from the teacher's work. The goal of the interview was to find out how these teachers know when they were doing a good job, how they dealt with the fact of their own power and that of their administrative superiors, and what pleasures, if any, life in the classroom held out to them. As the teachers responded to these three sets of questions their answers seemed to contain three or four recurrent themes that were more general than the questions themselves and, thus, provided a useful way of organizing the interview material. These themes, each of which concerns an aspect of classroom life felt to be desirable or necessary for the fulfillment of teaching duties, will be used in combination with the questions themselves in the discussion that follows. Although the complexity of each theme defies a brief description, four one-word labels are offered as aids to memory. These are *immediacy, informality, autonomy,* and *individuality.* Each of these themes will be treated separately in the material to follow. The last section of this chapter contains a discussion of all four themes and their educational implications.

I

The *immediacy* of classroom events is something that anyone who has ever been in charge of a roomful of students can never forget. There is a here-and-now urgency and a spontaneous quality that brings excitement and variety to the teacher's work, though it also may contribute to the fatigue he feels at the end of the day.

Although teaching might be thought of as being chiefly concerned with cognitive reorganization—with producing invisible changes within the student—this select group of teachers did not rely very much on pious hopes of reaping an "unseen harvest." In their view the results of teaching were quite visible. One aspect of this immediacy particularly evident in the reports of our teachers was the extent to which they used fleeting behavioral cues to tell them how well they were doing their jobs. The following brief interchange between the interviewer and an eighth grade teacher illustrates this tendency.

> INTERVIEWER: How can you tell when you're doing a good job?
>
> TEACHER: Oh, look at their faces.
>
> INTERVIEWER: Will you tell me more about that.
>
> TEACHER: Why, sure, they look alert; they look interested; they look questioning—like they're ready to question something. They look like they're anxious to learn more about it . . . And other times you know you haven't done a good job when they look blah or look disinterested or I-don't-care attitude, well then I feel bad, you know, I've done a bad job.

Another teacher tries to put her finger on the signs that tell her when one of her lessons has gone particularly well and ends, as did many others, by mentioning the visible signs of alertness and enthusiasm.

> The reaction, I think, of the children, and what they seem to have gained from it. Their interest; their expressions; the way they look.

A third interviewee, who teaches in the middle grades, reported this example of intellectual discovery and its facial consequences.

> . . . the day we were talking about (language) one of them wondered, came up later and said, "If we didn't have words, there'd be no knowledge and we couldn't tell anybody anything. All we could do is feel." And you could just tell from the look on her face that this whole thing suddenly had dawned on her.

One teacher with sixteen years of experience, all of them with fourth graders, claims to rely more on sound than on sight. She puts the matter this way.

I can tell by the way they sound. There is a sound that you can tell, and you can tell when they're really working.

INTERVIEWER: You mean the sound of the room in general?

TEACHER: The sound of the room in general. Now it doesn't always have to be a quiet sound—It can be a noisy, buzzing sound, and you're still doing a good job, and everybody's working.

INTERVIEWER: But can you tell?

TEACHER: I can tell. You can feel it.

A man who began his teaching career in high school and who is now teaching in the fifth grade sees a parallel between the actor's sensitivity to his audience and the teacher's responsiveness to subtle changes in his students. For this teacher the determination of his effectiveness is not difficult at all.

It's the easiest thing in the world. You know you're missing at the first yawn. Teaching and learning, if they're not enjoyable and fun, are both very difficult to accomplish. When the kids aren't having a good time, if they're not paying attention and sitting up, that's it—A theatrical sense is something that you can't learn, but a good actor can sense his audience. He knows when a performance is going well or not going well, simply by the feeling in the air. And it's that way in the classroom. You can feel when the kids are resistant.

Of course the teacher's interpretation of these signs is not infallible, as is indicated by the following comment from a teacher who was asked how she knew when she was doing a good job.

It's a feeling, also, as I said before. And maybe I am overly enthusiastic. I may not be reaching them. I may just be elated and think, "Boy, that's great!" and then when I get down, they may be sitting there thinking "What's she doing?"

One of our interviewees, a woman who has spent seven years with first graders, comments on a subtle distinction between behavior that indicates the absence of enthusiasm and that which arouses the suspicion of real learning difficulties. As she puts it,

First of all, I think there's a difference between their liking what you're doing and their learning what you're teaching. Sometimes they can like it immensely and not be learning a thing. You can tell when they're enthusiastic but you have to ask a few questions to know whether they're learning or not. In the first grade, if they don't *like* what you're doing, they will usually tell you so. They'll say "I don't want to do this anymore," or "When are we going home?" or something like this. They're very honest. But if they don't *understand* what you're doing, they usually won't express it verbally. They will climb on the desk or under the chair or make some quiet attempt to escape. They obviously don't want to have anything to do with the whole idea. Or else, if you question them, they'll know the answer, but not be very enthusiastic. They become very passive and usually don't cause you any trouble, but you know that they just aren't paying any attention.

Somewhat less fleeting than alert expressions and raised hands are indications that the student is willing to work above and beyond minimal expectations. These signs of a more enduring interest appear in a variety of forms, as the following set of comments from four of the interviewees indicate.

> They bring things to you like articles out of magazines or pictures they have drawn. For science or geography, they'll draw maps. To me, that shows they must be interested. Also they'll ask me for extra things they can do.

> Oh, another way you know is whether or not they bring slides, whether they bring in little pamphlets from the World's Fair for current events. Also visitors are an indication. One student has a cousin from out of town and asks "Could she please stay here for the morning?" You figure you've got something. Of course, maybe the mother wanted to get rid of the child for the morning. But there are parents who come in to school too because the child wants them to see what we're doing.

> I know I have caught their interest if they bring the things in that they need for experiments in science.

> If I have encouraged them to do more than the textbook readings in the basic text—if they have gone out into other books and tried to find pictures and other information, then I feel that they are interested in the subject.

As a group, the interview excerpts that have been presented thus far call attention to a puzzling feature of the relationship between the teacher's work and broader educational goals. From one point of view the school is properly described as a future-oriented institution. Its ultimate concern is with the future well-being of its clientele. A few educators may not like this description and may insist that school is life, and vice versa. But the preparatory function of school is hard to deny even in the earliest grades where the chief goal of education seems to be "enjoy, enjoy." Yet if we believe the testimony of these experienced teachers it is today's behavior rather than tomorrow's test that provides the real yardstick for measuring the teacher's progress. In fact, the attitude of these teachers toward tests and testing is sufficiently important to warrant special discussion.

In the most global terms, the goal of the schools is to promote learning. Thus, ideally we might expect teachers to derive a major source of their satisfactions from observing growth in achievement among their students. Further, the students' performance on tests of achievement (commercial or teacher-made) would seem to provide objective and readily obtainable evidence of this growth. Logically at least, the conscientious teacher ought to point with pride or disappointment to the gains or losses of students as measured by test performance. But, as is often true in human affairs, the logical did not occur. One of the most interesting features of the interview material was the absence of reference to objective evidence of school learning in contexts in which one might expect it to be discussed.

Testing, when it is mentioned at all, is given little emphasis. These teachers treat it as being of minor importance in helping them understand how well they have done.

The students' enthusiasm and involvement seem much more important than do their performance on tests, as is evident in the following comment by a fourth grade teacher who is identifying the evidence of effectiveness on which she typically relies.

> I know I'm getting through when the kids are sparking and interested and excited in what they're doing. I think it's the feeling of the class and it's the way the class behaves. I don't think you can tell off in a vacuum, and I don't think you can tell by the objectives, and I don't think you can tell by the tests. It's the degree to which the kids feel part of the activities of the room and participate in them with pleasure.

The most enthusiastic statement about testing in the entire set of interviews was the following from a fifth grade teacher who described how she knew when she was doing a good job.

> I don't rely entirely on tests. I use tests at the beginning of the year to find out what they know. Then, as the year

progresses I can tell how much they are learning by their attitudes and by their notebooks. I rely quite a bit on the notebooks. Occasionally I give a test, but I judge their progress by these other things too.

Several reasons for the teacher's avoidance of paper-and-pencil tests are hinted at by the teachers. In the very early grades, for example, there are few commercial tests available even if the teacher wanted to use this kind of formal evaluation. As a second grade teacher put it,

> As far as the second grade goes, there really isn't any testing. You can make up your own little exams but there is no good standard test. The *Iowa Test* is given in third grade, but the results don't mean anything until the child has taken it again in the fourth grade. You have to wait a year before you can tell anything from it.

In schools having a formal achievement testing program, the results, if they are ever reported to the teacher, arrive too late to do much good. When asked whether she used objective achievement data provided by the central office, one teacher commented,

> I'm always very anxious to see the standardized scores and see how the kids made out. But they come out at the end of the year and by that time it's too late to do anything about it. That's one of the things.
>
> INTERVIEWER: But might it affect what you do with the next group?
>
> TEACHER: With the next class? Not terribly.

From a psychological viewpoint, however, the scarcity of useful instruments and poor administrative practices in handling them are not as important as is a general distrust of tests that was evident in several of the interviews. Two major forms of this distrust can be identified. First is the belief that children behave atypically on tests; that test information often does not confirm the teacher's judgment derived from her classroom contacts. Furthermore, when these contradictions between test scores and teacher judgment occur, the teacher seems more likely to deny the accuracy of the test information than to alter her previous assessment of the student. The following set of remarks typify this point of view.

> I give written tests, but I don't count heavily on them. In my own personal experience, I've known a subject and not done well on a test on it. I stress oral participation in class and I can tell whether they are interested or not.

Tests, of course, will help some, but I don't think the child always responds on a test so that you can tell exactly what progress he's made. A lot of them just never do well on a test even though on their daily work they show that they're making progress. You can judge progress by changes in their attitudes too. They have so many dislikes —"I don't like this" or "I can't do this." When their attitude begins to change and they *do* like what they are doing and they *can* do it, then I feel that they're making progress.

At times it's discouraging, because I feel that I have covered the material very thoroughly, but I give a test and see the scores and think, "Oh, my! Didn't I teach any better than this?" And then I stop and think, well, they have certainly learned more than they knew before, and you can't expect them to get every little detail. . . .

A second form of distrust is represented by the suspicion that performance on achievement tests is more a reflection of native ability than of teaching effectiveness. Thus, when annual gains or losses are observed they are often interpreted as "natural" phenomena whose informational value to the teacher is very small. A third grade teacher puts the matter this way:

Of course, the achievement grades mean something, but then you can't compare this classroom's results with another classroom's results because you have entirely different children. I don't think we should judge accomplishment by the test results. I so well recall the class that I had that went all the way from 3-1 to 4-2, workbook and all, and still had time left over. I've never had a class like it—since or before. I would hate to have that class's achievement records put beside, let's say last year's, which wasn't very good. District-wise and national-wise last year's achievement records were all right. But if you put the test records of those two classes side by side, I either didn't do a good job last year or I did an outstanding job that other year. And it wasn't that. It's just that I had the material to work with. That was all.

A fourth grade teacher made the following comment when asked to describe the conditions under which her teaching behavior would be influenced by the test performance of her students.

It would if, for instance, all my kids had low reading scores. This isn't going to happen. I mean, it may not have any thing to do with the teacher when that happens.

In the extreme case, objective testing is perceived as being under the control of the authorities, completely unconnected with teaching objectives and with the routine of the classroom. When this point of view is present, it is hardly surprising to find the teacher looking upon testing as if it were just a nuisance.

126

> I was very upset that I had to spend an hour on standardized testing to find out whether or not they know the math. It was just for the SMSG book. I know what they know. It's a survey, so we have to do it.

> Today was a very tiring day because the children were tested this morning. Actually I didn't do much; I graded their papers and that's it. I'd rather have an active day. I think I'm more tired after a day of doing nothing.

Thus, the interview excerpts give the impression that the outstanding elementary teacher does not often turn to objective measures of school achievement for evidence of his effectiveness and as a source of professional satisfaction. Rather, the question of how well he is doing seems to be answered by the continual flow of information from the students during the teaching session. Spontaneous expressions of interest and enthusiasm are among the most highly valued indicators of good teaching, although the quality of the students' contributions to daily sessions is also mentioned frequently.

The attitude of these teachers toward testing and their reliance on fleeting behavioral cues combine to create a seeming paradox: present-oriented teachers in future-oriented institutions. Or is this as paradoxical as it first seems? Does the teacher's focus on today necessarily conflict with the school's focus on tomorrow? The answer, it would seem, is "No, not necessarily." Apparently teachers can and do give tests and keep an eye on long-range goals while concentrating on the immediate signs of student involvement and enthusiasm. Yet the fact that such a dual focus is possible suggests that it might become a source of discomfort for the teacher under certain circumstances. Our interview material reveals some signs of this discomfort even among teachers who have achieved an enviable reputation in their school systems.

II

A second theme in the interview material, one which has been labelled *informality,* is evident at two points in the comments of many teachers. It first appears in the descriptions the teachers give of their teaching style. Most frequently when asked to describe their distinctive ways of working with children, the teachers focused on the relative degree of formality or informality characterizing their daily work. For several teachers the broad question of style seemed to boil down to the narrower question of how they used their authority in the classroom. A young teacher who works with second graders was succinct in her response to our query about teaching style.

> I'd say I was very casual with the children, and I use a subtle, even sarcastic approach with them if I find it necessary.

Often our interviewees would compare their way of working with that of "old-fashioned" teachers or teachers whom they had had during their own childhood. As might be expected, these comparisons usually focused on the greater freedom and informality in the interviewee's classroom. The following response from a fifth-grade teacher is typical:

> I just have a very free and friendly attitude toward the children. It's much different from the old-fashioned type of teaching that I had when I was a kid, it really is. This school is quite a nice school to teach in; the children are very receptive to learning. So it's probably easier to be that way here than it would be in some places. . . .

> I would just say that I have to have a lot of freedom in the way that I teach because each class is different. It takes each class a different length of time to learn something that you're presenting to them. I do a lot of speaking myself, oral presentation, but not formal lectures. I try to maintain a very informal atmosphere and there's a lot of jumping around that goes along with it to keep the interest of the children. . . .

A veteran of forty years in elementary classrooms describes her style in this way,

> I think that in the classroom I try to be informal. I mean, I try to make this situation as much as possible like a family group sitting around a fireplace or around a table when some question has come up and they're discussing it. Now of course I believe in having discipline but it isn't the kind of authoritarian discipline that teachers practiced years ago, for instance, when my mother was teaching. But on the other hand I want the child to feel free sometimes to say, "I disagree with you" or "I think you've made a mistake." I want to feel that any time I can say

to the children, "I'm not certain about something and I would like to look it up." I don't want the children in my room to feel nervous about their work; I don't want the nerves in the back of their necks to become tense. If a child is performing commensurate with his ability, that's the most that I expect from each one.

The second point at which informality was mentioned by several of the interviewees was when they were asked to describe how their teaching had changed with time. Some, usually the more inexperienced teachers, focused on changes over relatively brief periods. For example, one fifth grade teacher said,

> My teaching is always more structured, more rigid at the beginning of the school year than it is later as I get to know the class. You have to know the class first before you can be relaxed and casual.

Others chose to focus on changes spanning their entire teaching career. For these teachers as well, the formality-informality dimension was frequently prominent, as in the following response from another fifth grade teacher,

> I think I've moved more from being a formal type of teacher into a more informal one. At the beginning of my teaching experience I was very concerned with being able to control my class. Many times I would feel that perhaps I would lose my discipline if I were more informal with the children and allowed them more freedom. Also I just didn't know the limits I could set for the children or how far they would go. I didn't know what limits were reasonable. After I became more accustomed to the typical behavior of children of this age, why it was easier for me to set less rigid limits.

These mentions of informality probably do not come as a surprise to anyone who has spent much time in modern elementary schools, particularly those in suburban communities. The hallmarks of today's classroom are the movable desks and the collapsible walls, with the concomitant social movement each affords. Gone are the fixed rows and frozen postures of yesterday. But the apparent informality is a relative matter at best. Its meaning is derived from a comparison of what teaching once was or what it might become if the teacher chose to exercise the full power of his authority. "Informal," as these teachers use the term, really means *less* formal rather than *not* formal, for even in the most up-to-date classroom much that goes on is still done in accordance with forms, rules, and conventions.

Today's teachers may exercise their authority more casually than did their predecessors, and they may unbend increasingly with experience, but there are real limits to how far they can move in this direction. As a group, our interviewees clearly recognized and respected those limits. For them, the desire for informality was never sufficiently strong to interfere with institutional definitions of responsibility, authority, and tradition.

III

The third theme identified in our interviews had to do with the teacher's perception of his own professional *autonomy*. This theme is similar to the theme of informality but instead of focusing on the teacher's relation with his students it concerns his relation with his own superiors. Here too, apparently, there exists greater rigidity and formality than is desired.

Our interviewees mentioned two main threats to the teacher's autonomy, or at least two hypothetical conditions, which, if either materialized, would arouse complaint: one concerned the possibility of an inflexible curriculum; the other concerned the possible invasion of the classroom by administrative superiors bent on evaluation. Our teachers were quite emphatic about what they would do under the first of these conditions. A fifth-grade teacher, for example, became increasingly perturbed as he contemplated the potential loss of his autonomy.

> If I were given a curriculum guide and a series of lesson plans that said "You will teach this way; you will teach this material at this time and take so long to do it," if they made teaching too rigid or started telling me that I must use this book or that book and could not bring in supplementary materials of my own, and then I'd quit. Forget it! You can hire an orangutan to come in and pass out books. You really can! I'd walk out the door tomorrow.

It was not only male teachers who winced at the thought of too many curricular constraints. Many of the women were equally concerned. For example, one female interviewee confessed,

> . . . I moved from another system to this system for that very reason. There was so much supervision and so much "We will all be on page so-and-so in such-and-such a book on such-and-such a day." I don't see how you can teach that way because people are not like that. As long as you've

got ten different teachers teaching the same grade you are going to have it taught ten different ways, and yet the children are going to come out at the end of the year having gotten a great deal out of it. Ten different people present things in ten different ways because they *are* ten different individuals.

A fourth grade teacher with a decade of experience was equally adamant when asked to consider the possibility of increased restrictions in her choice of teaching materials. She first blurted out, "I'd get fired! I wouldn't do it!" and then went on to describe an incident that had occurred in her own school.

> An example is this math which we teachers feel is not properly programmed for fourth grade. We recently got together the fourth grade teachers and cut out what we didn't think the bulk of the students could handle and we told our principal what we had done. Now if he had said, "You can't do that. You've got to teach this," I'd have said, "Well, you need a new teacher." This would have been my attitude. I would be most uncomfortable in that kind of situation—if I felt I had to keep the job, I think I would be miserable.

Another fourth grade teacher tried to be as specific as possible in explaining to the interviewer what she would not like, and why.

> I would be bothered if I were told that I had to have arithmetic from nine to nine-thirty and spelling from nine-thirty to nine-forty-five. I think it's good to have a schedule but I would hate for them to say, "Now, if we come in your room at nine-thirty, that's what we want to see you teaching." Yes, that would bother me. I wouldn't like that at all. I certainly would not. That wouldn't be very flexible, would it? That's what I like to be. Suppose the children say to me, "Oh, Mrs. ——, here's a song that we learned in the beginning of the year." It's in a book that they're reading. I'll say, "Well, I hadn't thought about that song in a long time. Let's sing it." So we're in the middle of reading and we'll stop and sing this song. And they love that. You can see their little bodies slink back and relax. And, you know, it gets the crick out of my back, too.

Closely related to the threat of too many curricular controls is the requirement of having the classroom teacher plan his work far in advance. This practice was clearly distasteful to several of the interviewees. As one veteran of twenty-nine years in the classroom put it,

> In neighboring districts, teachers have to have lesson plans made for nine weeks ahead of time and they have to be checked through. I don't believe I've made a lesson plan since I did my practice teaching. So I suppose if I ended up with a supervisor or principal that wanted lesson plans for nine weeks, it would shake me up. I'd probably get something down on paper; whether I'd follow it through or not I don't know. That would be something else.

There are two sources of uneasiness embedded in these complaints. One is the fear that the spontaneity of the classroom would be destroyed by too many constraints; the other is the hurt created by an implied insult to the teacher's professional pride. These two concerns are both present in the following statement from a second-grade teacher.

> I think that it's important that a teacher is respected for her own ideas about teaching and isn't told how to do it. I personally wouldn't like to be handed a curriculum guide and told "Follow it." I like to do what I want to do when I want to do it. I have friends in other systems who have to turn in lesson plans a week or a month in advance. To me this is silly, because you don't teach that way. If something interesting comes up, a butterfly flies in the window, we talk about butterflies. I do make a lesson plan out every week and Monday morning I stick to it from nine to ten, but by ten o'clock I'm usually off of it. I have it there for a substitute, or for myself, if I'm really hard up for something to do I can look in my book and see what I planned to do. But I—that would be one thing that would really annoy me.

The teacher's uneasiness over the prospect of being observed too frequently also is linked to his feelings of professional pride. The same second-grade teacher who just argued for the freedom to deal with the unexpected intrusion of a butterfly becomes quite upset when the intruder is a fellow human from the central office, as the following comment indicates.

> I hate to be observed. I would hate to have the principal or superintendent or somebody bugging me all the time. I think —— is an unusual system where we are very seldom observed. I sometimes used to wonder how I was doing. Now I don't because I'm confident. I know I'm

doing a fairly good job because I haven't had to retain too many students and the third grade teachers don't complain too much. But I often wondered at the beginning if they knew what I was doing. I could have been in there playing tiddledywinks. But I think they pride themselves on their original selection. I think that they feel they've weeded people out pretty carefully. I work better if I'm not checked up on. I would have guilt feelings if I didn't do enough work. But if someone were checking up on me, it'd work the other way. I'm just stubborn enough that I'd say, "Okay, come and watch and I won't do anything." That's one thing that would bother me about a system.

Apparently the intention of the visitors, their desire to "check-up," disturbs the teacher more than does their actual physical presence. As one teacher puts it,

It doesn't bother me having people go in and out of the room, but it does bother me to have people come in and sit down and take notes. And that's another reason why I moved from that school.

INTERVIEWER: Why did that bother you?

TEACHER: I suppose because I feel they're going to criticize me. I don't know. It isn't because I can't take criticism, either, but it just does bother me to have people sit and write and take notes while I'm there, watching me.

A few of our teachers were so strongly opposed to the idea of being evaluated that they threatened to leave the classroom rather than withstand an outsider's critical glance. This attitude is particularly significant when we recall the professional status of our interviewees. These teachers, it must be remembered, were described as outstanding by their superiors. Supposedly they have the least to hide and the most to gain from the visit of an evaluator. Yet even the knowledge that they are well-thought-of does not allay the concerns of some. As an instance, a first-grade teacher who has spent most of her lifetime working with children and who, therefore, might be expected to be among the last to contemplate leaving her chosen profession, was quick to say,

If I knew I had to face merit-rating I think that would make me get out immediately. Because—well various reasons. But in our district we are free to do what we think is right for the different grade levels.

Apparently these teachers feel most comfortable with the classroom door closed and the curriculum guides tucked away in the supplies closet. But their concern over the preservation of professional autonomy must not be misinterpreted as reflecting a desire for isolation and total independence. These teachers are not complaining about the togetherness of institutional living. They do not want to be alone with their roomful of pupils; they merely want to be free from inspection while performing certain of their duties. As a matter of fact, our interviews contain many indications of a desire to draw more heavily than they presently do on the services of other specialists within the system—such as music and art teachers. In other words, these teachers are not asking for a return to the isolated conditions of the one-room school. They want company and they want help, but they also want to preserve the feeling of being on their own in the classroom.

A similar complexity is found in their attitude toward a prescribed curriculum. Again, no one indicated the desire to construct his own educational program from scratch. All seemed quite willing to accept the guidelines set down by the curriculum committees and textbook manufacturers. But inside these guidelines they wanted room for spontaneity and the exercise of professional judgment. Here again, as was true of their desire for informality, the teacher's plea was for freedom, but freedom *within limits*.

IV

The fourth theme detected in the interviews is summarized by the word *individuality*. It deals with the teacher's interest in the well-being of individual students in his class and becomes particularly evident when the teacher is asked to describe the satisfactions he derives from his work. Although he confronts an entire class, it is what happens to individuals that really counts. As one teacher puts it,

> I think that the thing that perhaps keeps me in teaching is, not *all* those twenty-five or thirty kids that you have each year, but those one or two that finally, all of a sudden begin to see through things and have the world open up to them. I think that that's the thing—that, and the appreciations that you get from some children and from their families from year to year. The blossoming of a slow child, or of a shy child is—well, just seems to make it all worthwhile.

Though fleeting signs of student attention and involvement doubtlessly are gratifying to the teacher, they are not the greatest satisfactions that life in the classroom has to offer. The joys of teaching—and, at least for this group of devoted professionals, "joys" is a more accurate word than "satisfactions"—the joys of teaching are many. They are not limited, as we have seen, to the official business of achieving educational objectives (though that may account for a part of them). Instead they reflect the variety of responsibilities and opportunities that comprise the role of the elementary school teacher. Moreover, they are closely tied to what the teacher sees happening to individual students. One way of organizing this assortment of pleasures is to order them in terms of the intensity of emotional involvement each entails.

134

At one extreme would be the continual satisfaction, usually of low intensity, that comes from thinking of oneself as serving a good cause. A sense of personal usefulness comes closest to describing this class of satisfactions. As one suburban teacher puts it,

> I think it's like missionary work. I've always been very socially-minded, and I think that we really do have a lot of work to do right in these communities, not just in the underprivileged ones.

A distinguishing feature of the elementary teacher's missionary work is, of course, the age of its beneficiaries. The teacher not only helps people, she helps them at the most crucial time of their lives— when they are young.

The following comment from a second grade teacher contains a realization of the potency of the early years in giving shape to later development.

> I think when you're helping young people, and—I don't know, it's rather hard to answer—you're teaching them something new all the time, you're helping them to develop. Especially down at this age, if they do not get a good background—this is my feeling anyway—if they do not have a good background by the time they come out of second grade, they will have trouble going on.

Underlying the sense of usefulness, then, is a spirit of urgency. Like the missionary, the teacher has only a limited time to complete his work. Moreover, if he does not succeed, the ill effects may be irreparable. The possibility of failure, of time running out, and of wasted efforts introduces an element of risk to the teacher's task that is absent in many of the more casual forms of social service— such as the ladies aid volunteers. Also, the fact that the teacher might fail means, of course, that he might succeed. His perception of student progress, as informal indicator of his success, is mentioned by several teachers as an important source of satisfaction providing a more intense emotional experience than those derived from the mere fact of membership in a good cause. The following set of quotations epitomize this point of view.

> Let's see, the rewards. I think just seeing them happy and seeing them progress is the biggest reward.

> Seeing a child be successful is reward enough. I think this is the thing we are striving for, really, in education. We want to see a child find his place in life and be successful, and when he's on the road to this, even in school, we're happy. We watch, at least I do watch my youngsters as they go along and progress. I check up with the fourth grade teachers and see whether or not there are strengths or weaknesses or things that I should have been doing with them to help them along the way.

> The children's progress is a reward for me. I try to keep a very close check as to how they're getting along. If I have a child that comes in in the fall with many problems, many difficulties, and he overcomes some of those, then I feel that we're making progress and we're getting someplace.

> I get a bang out of seeing their faces light up with an idea or a sense of accomplishment.

In the last quotation the words "bang" and "light up" call attention to a characteristic of classroom life that provides an additional source of emotional arousal and satisfaction: the frequent occurrence of unexpected events. The fact that no one can predict with great accuracy what a day's teaching holds in store creates, at least for the teacher who craves variety, an atmosphere of pleasant anticipation about her work, perhaps even excitement. This feeling is well expressed in the following quotation from a third grade teacher.

> I just wish that everyone could feel the excitement that there is in teaching—the eagerness to get into the classroom. It's the strangest thing . . . that no matter if you're sad or if you don't feel well, or if things aren't the rosiest, you can come into the classroom in the morning and a child will come up and everything is all right. Because you're needed. Maybe the child is sad and you forget your troubles or maybe he has come in with something he just has to tell you and it's just the biggest thing in the world. All of a sudden, you know, you forget your problems. I

just wonder if there are other occupations like this, where people find the same gratification.

Elements of the unexpected and of surprise are also prominent in the following statements from two men. The first teaches a fifth grade class and the second works with eighth graders.

> Oh—well, I've mentioned some of the excitements of teaching: class discussion that veers in a surprising direction, that you never thought it'd go and goes higher than you ever dreamed possible; a child who never had any ideas that showed who suddenly makes an observation that brings two things together, "That's just like this." Sometimes one kid suddenly makes a spurt and does something that you never thought he could do. Sometimes it's a whole class that does something together that you never thought a class could do. One time a little fifth grade girl came up after class and said, "I just learned how to divide." That was that day—it was that class period. I don't know how it happened, but it happened.

> Of course you get rewards—at least I feel that I get rewards every day. Perhaps, having a small class that I can observe closely, I can see improvement better than a teacher with a larger class. But hardly a day goes by but some student who hasn't been doing so well or one that may have been doing quite well, grasps something different, or gets that little twinkle in his eye and—for once, he's achieved something that, maybe, he didn't think he could, and this is a reward for me.

Of course surprising and unexpected classroom events do not always have to do with the attainment of learning goals. Sometimes a student's behavior is just plain amusing or entertaining, and has little or no relevance to educational matters.

> Oh, I enjoy children's reactions to things, and the things that they say or do. They're so funny sometimes, I have wished that I had time to write a book, but you can't put them down on paper and make them sound as funny as they really are when they happen.

The unexpected events of the classroom vary considerably in size and importance, from small happenings that are often merely funny or annoying to great leaps of progress and motivational awakenings. The more dramatic transformations, which in some ways resemble acts of religious conversion, are yet another source of satisfaction for the teacher to experience—at a deeper level of emotion than those already described. If unexpected events in general bring excitement to the teacher's work, these classroom "miracles," which are of major proportions and of great psychological significance, afford the teacher who is fortunate enough to witness them, something close to a thrill.

In their descriptions the teachers often use literary devices, such as metaphor and simile, to emphasize the dramatic and almost magical quality of some of these transformations. The students in question don't simply change for the better, they "see the light of day," they "wake up," they become "uncorked," and so forth. The following set of comments from three seasoned teachers illustrates the use of metaphorical expressions to describe what happens in class.

> There are the advanced ones, whom you see you have helped advance more. There are the very very slow ones who all of a sudden see the light of day, and you feel that you've shown them the way. Even if it was just their own development, you give yourself credit.

> I think I have satisfaction seeing someone progress, especially a slow child or an average child who all of a sudden comes out, maybe in the middle. I had a boy in here at the beginning of the semester who wouldn't work. He'd just sit. He's very intelligent, on the verge of being a genius I understand, but he wrote like a second grader, wouldn't bother doing work, would forget things. This went on and on. Then he was sick and was absent and after he came back in January, all of a sudden he was a different boy. He's got average handwriting now, but he finishes everything. He gets almost straight A's. It's a satisfaction that maybe I have gotten across to him; on the other hand, maybe it's him, maybe he just woke up.

> Let me cite one case specifically where a child did a series of triangles and thought it was beautiful but it wasn't beautiful. I asked her to use her eyes and observe and see if she could make it better. She was quite agreeable to looking out the window and looking at the forms that windows make and the forms that a building makes, and we worked on her drawing. I don't think I've ever seen a more thrilled face than when she realized that she could do something to make that drawing more interesting. She became uncorked.

Dramatic changes do not take place, of course, within every student. But the few that do occur are sufficient compensation for the hours spent in front of a blackboard. A first grade teacher makes this point clear.

138

> When you see a child that has suddenly caught on and is enjoying reading or is going ahead to be an independent worker, you can't help but have satisfaction and know that you have done something for this particular child. You know that you aren't going to do wonders with every child because children—some of them just don't hit maturity until second or third grade. But when you do see a child bloom, it's gratifying.

The sources of satisfaction discussed thus far have been presented in order of increasing emotional intensity—from a sense of personal usefulness, to a feeling of accomplishment, to excitement created by the unexpected, to the thrill of witnessing dramatic change. The most dramatic change of all and, hence, one of the greatest thrills of teaching occurs when the person who changes is a student whom other teachers, or adults in general, have given up for lost. This situation, which is epitomized in the story of Helen Keller's childhood, and which was so movingly portrayed in the play and movie, "The Miracle Worker" might not happen too often, but when it does it is memorable, as the following comment indicates.

> When you've had a child who has been a severe problem and some way you've reached him and done something for him, that's a real thrill. I just don't think there's any other job that provides you with the depth of feeling that you have in a situation like this. Oh, perhaps a doctor, when he saves a life has such a feeling. But I think in most professions, they don't have such experiences. It's almost a spiritual feeling that you get when you've had a success reaching such a child and helping him.

Because these transformations cannot be accurately predicted, and because they sometimes seem to happen despite, rather than as a result of, what anyone has done to the student, it is impossible to give credit for their occurrence with much certainty. Nevertheless, their unpredictability neither dulls the teacher's enjoyment of these events, nor discourages him from taking at least partial credit for them.

> It's a real satisfaction to see someone make a great step forward. I mentioned a little girl I have who was particularly unresponsive. At the first of the year I thought she wasn't getting anywhere and I was about to give up on her. Now she's doing well, especially in science. I

think I want to take a part of that credit, but maybe she'd have done it anyway. With these things you never know.

The desire to witness these most moving of all classroom experiences, and possibly to have a hand in their occurrence, doubtlessly increases the attractiveness of troubled, "lost," unwanted children in the eyes of many teachers. When room assignments are made it is not unusual for a teacher to seek out such students for his class. In a sense, these youngsters are academic longshots: there is small chance of their ending in the money, but the assurance of an enormous emotional payoff to the teacher if they do. The reference to gambling must not leave the impression that the teacher is merely playing games—selfishly stacking the membership of his class to produce the biggest emotion "bang." But there is something attractive about the underdog, and many teachers feel an affection and closeness to these children quite unlike that which they feel toward the more "well-adjusted" or successful student. A fourth grade teacher makes this point quite clear.

> I have favorites as people. There are some kids who are just plain more attractive than others. And it's not always in terms of what a non-teacher would think attractive. I can find a kid with a lot of problems extremely attractive. Take Billy, for instance. I first saw this little bitty boy get up in front of a whole audience and make a fool of himself. Then I asked for him for my class. He is a thoroughly unattractive child in many, many ways. But I felt a kind of a bond with him just from watching everybody laughing and not being sure whether they were laughing with or at him. You see, there's this kind of attractiveness too.

For some teachers a sudden change in a child's behavior releases special feelings of warmth and affection.

> The little girl whose drawing I just described was colorless and I didn't have very much feeling for her for a long time. Then all of a sudden when she began to make discoveries, her personality popped out and I loved her.

The use of the word "love" in the above quotation introduces a source of satisfaction that transcends even the thrill of observing a student's metamorphosis. During their interviews many teachers, particularly the women, spoke of their deep affection for individual children. At this level of emotional attachment the role of teacher as teacher begins to blur and to merge with the role of mother. Occasionally a teacher referred specifically to the relationship between teaching and mothering, and spoke frankly and poignantly of the motives underlying her own behavior. The following comments are illustrative.

> A teacher has to find what age she enjoys—and I'm sure that depends on the personality of the teacher. For myself, I like mothering and so I like to teach the lower grades. Probably I feel this way because my husband and I never could have children of our own, much as we wanted to. I like the love and affection you get from the young children which I miss from children of my own. Probably another teacher who didn't have this need would enjoy teaching a little more stimulating material.

> For me, of course, it's working with the children that makes teaching rewarding. I am married, but do not have any children of my own and I feel that I get a lot from being with the children in my class. Contact with them is probably what I would miss most if I left teaching. Some of them become very close, and yet in teaching you just cannot treat one child differently from the other child. Still you can't help thinking, "If I had one, I would like it to be. . . ."

Not all teachers, of course, admit to feelings as deep as those discussed here. In fact, one teacher of the middle grades explicitly denied the appropriateness of the term "love" when used to describe her relationship with her students.

> I think I would call it respect rather than love or affection. Yes, I'd call it respect.

Yet this same teacher, when asked what the close of the school year was like, remarked,

> Sometimes I'm very unhappy at the end of the year because I'd like to teach the same class again. You become so attached to them sometimes that you just would enjoy continuing with the same group for another year.

The pain of separation was mentioned by several of the teachers. Although it is the opposite of satisfaction, this discomfort at the thought of the students' departure deserves mention because it attests to the closeness of the ties that develop, sometimes even against the teacher's will.

> Comes June and I hate to see these children go. You just get attached to them.

> In the beginning of the year for years I've resented the teacher who got the class I had had the year before. I can't

help thinking of them as my kids. However, as the years
go by I'm learning to live with this kind of thing.

I don't know just why, but I do get very attached to them
through the years. . . . One of the joys of the holiday
season is hearing from so many youngsters. Some of them
are now in high school.

As the preceding interview excerpt indicates, in a few happy
instances the teacher-pupil relationship never truly ends. The reward
of being remembered with affection by former students is important
to many teachers. Also, many continue to participate vicariously in
a student's accomplishments long after he has left the classroom. This
extension of the teacher-pupil relationship over time adds a final
(though somewhat milder) type of satisfaction to those already
discussed. The probability of deriving pleasure from the remem-
brances or achievements of former students obviously increases
with years of teaching experience.

I have had a lot of satisfaction in picking out youngsters who
probably would never have gone to college and encouraging them to go. I've loaded them in my car on Saturdays
and taken them to college campuses. I've helped them to
apply for whatever it was they had to apply for to get
them started in college. Yes, I've had some real rewards
doing that; one of those youngsters is a Ph.D. and is on
the faculty of —— now. I don't know, they might have all
gotten into college without me, it's hard to know. But
I've given myself some credit for their going.

In one year, I probably won't see any specific gains in the
youngsters but when my third graders go into fourth
grade, then I begin to see real progress and this gives me
great pleasure. Another pleasure is having students come
back to see me from high school, and from college. Some
of the youngsters who were no great shakes in third grade
have become valedictorians in their high school careers
and this makes me feel real good, that maybe a little of
what I tried to teach them has really rubbed off.

I like to think that whatever these kids become, I have put
my licks in somewhere along the line. That gives me a
terrific feeling of pride.

The focus on the individual and on the gratifications provided by
former students was amusingly described by an interviewee who
teaches English to seventh and eighth graders. This teacher, who has

spent more than thirty-five years at her work, is still puzzled from time to time about the motives that keep her coming back to the classroom each fall.

> I sometimes wonder what I do like about teaching. I suppose that in the long run I know honestly, and I hear from many students, that something has been accomplished. The glow from that feeling of accomplishment warms me up enough to keep me going on. Now granted in February when they're all monsters or they're out with the flu and I'm making up work, I can't see why I am teaching, frankly. But I suppose basically I like the children and basically I never give up hope, and I—I am enthusiastic every September. Why, I have no idea. But I get rather excited, and I look at this batch of new faces and I think, "Mercy!" But I can like them. I grow to like even the worst. I had three seniors come in to see me last night; they're graduated from high school, wanted to know if I remember them—How could I forget! Yes, I remembered them, remembered some of the things that had happened and felt good that they remembered and they came back to say so. I had one young man come in who is taking his master's degree in journalism. He asked if I remembered him in English. I could never forget him. He was the world's worst . . . I suppose it's those things that make teaching worthwhile.

Given the pleasure these teachers reportedly derive from the progress of particular students, we might begin to wonder whether they would prefer a one-to-one arrangement such as occurs in the tutorial form of instruction. After all, with only one student at a time to worry about the teacher might concentrate all of his energies on the task of producing a change of great magnitude. But the tutoring relationship was an unappealing alternative to our interviewees.

When asked what they believed the ideal teacher-student ratio to be, most of our teachers expressed a preference for a class of 20 to 25 students. The suggestion of a class with 10 or fewer students met with almost unanimous rejection. The specific reasons for this rejection varied somewhat from teacher to teacher but the underlying idea was shared by many. The teachers complained that the small group would not offer enough stimulation or "give-and-take." One talked about needing a larger group to facilitate "the intermingling of personalities"; another argued that there would not be enough competition if the number of students became too small. A fourth grade teacher summed up the opinion of many when she said, "There's a certain spark that you lose if you have too few."

Thus, paralleling the teacher's delight in observing the progress of individuals is his insistence on having a group with which to work. At first glance these conditions may appear contradictory, but on further reflection the apparent contradiction disappears. These teachers are not asking for a group in the usual social or psychological sense of the term. They do not talk about their class as if it comprised a social unit with integrated parts and differentiated functions. Rather they seem to be calling for a collection of individuals, a collection large enough to "keep things moving" and small enough to preserve the visibility of individual members. Stable social relations commonly develop within these collections of students and some classes surely evolve into groups in the functional sense of the term. But the primary unit of the elementary school teacher's concern and the major source of his satisfaction remains the individual and his development.

V

Having identified the broad themes around which the talks with teachers seemed to revolve, there remains the task of considering the general relevance of the interview material for an understanding of life in classrooms. In doing so it will be necessary to touch upon aspects of the interviews that have only been briefly mentioned as well as those about which there has already been extensive discussion. The conversations of the teachers bear broadly on two topics: the conditions of teaching, and the general psychology of those adults who choose to work in elementary schools. These two topics are related, in turn, to the general question of how individuals, adults and children alike, come to grips with the demands of institutional life.

One of the most notable features of teacher talk is the absence of a technical vocabulary. Unlike professional encounters between doctors, lawyers, garage mechanics, and astrophysicists, when teachers talk together almost any reasonably intelligent adult can listen in and comprehend what is being said. Occasionally familiar words are used in a specialized sense, and the uninitiated listener may be momentarily puzzled by the mention of "units," or "projects," or "curriculum guides," or "word attack skills," but it is unlikely he will encounter many words that he has never heard before or even those with a specialized meaning.[4]

---

[4] This quality of teacher language has also been noted by my colleague Professor Dan Lortie. See, for example, his article "Teacher socialization: the Robinson Crusoe model," in *The Real World of the Beginning Teacher* (Washington, D.C.: National Education Association, 1966), pp. 54–66.

Not only is there an absence of a technical vocabulary unique to teaching, but also little use is made of jargon from related fields. A few psychological expressions are used from time to time (IQ is doubtlessly the most popular), but technical terms from the literature of psychopathology, group dynamics, learning theory, social organization, and developmental psychology—to name only the more obvious supporting disciplines—are noticeably absent. Teachers rarely talk about defense mechanisms, group cohesiveness, reinforcement schedules, role expectations, and sociocentric stages, even when it might be appropriate for them to do so.

The absence of technical terms is related to another characteristic of teachers' talk: its conceptual simplicity. Not only do teachers avoid elaborate words, they also seem to shun elaborate ideas. Obviously, this characteristic is not unique to teachers. Complicated thought is difficult and most people avoid it when they can, but such an avoidance (if that is what it should be called) does take on a special significance when we consider the importance of the teacher's work. Superficially at least, it would seem as if the thinking of teachers ought to be as complex as they can make it, as they set about the serious business of helping students to learn. Unnecessary simplicity, therefore, when revealed in the language of a teacher, would be interpreted by many as a cause for alarm. Whether or not that alarm is justified is a question to which we shall return.

Four aspects of the conceptual simplicity revealed in teachers' language are worthy of comment. These are: 1) an uncomplicated view of causality; 2) an intuitive, rather than rational approach to classroom events; 3) an opinionated, as opposed to an open-minded, stance when confronted with alternative teaching practices; and 4) a narrowness in the working definitions assigned to abstract terms.

When discussing the events with which they are confronted daily, teachers often talk as if theirs was a world in which single causes typically produced single effects. As they struggle to explain a puzzling classroom episode they commonly settle on what they consider to be *the* explanation. Why is Billy doing so well in school? Because he has a high IQ. Why is Fred such a trouble-maker? Because he comes from a broken family. Why are the children so noisy today? Because it's getting near the Christmas holiday. Even their own behavior as teachers is approached as if there were some kind of a one-to-one correspondence between cause and effect. Why, for example, did they choose to become teachers in the first place? The answer is obvious. Because they like children. Why else?

It is easy, of course, to make fun of these oversimplifications, but the complexity underlying most classroom events is so great that the teacher's search for a quick resolution of this complexity is understandable, perhaps even forgiveable. Were she seriously to try untangling the web of forces that combine to produce reality as she knows it, there would be no time for anything else. Moreover, when all is said and done, who does know for certain why Billy performs so well in school or why Miss Jones has elected to spend her life in a kindergarten? The assignment of single causes to these events is short-sighted, to be sure, but it does bring some semblance of order to an otherwise confusing and often chaotic environment.

Their willingness to accept simple explanations for complex events does not mean that teachers commonly insist on explanations for everything they witness. On the contrary, they are unusually willing to accept things as they are without probing too deeply into the whys and wherefores. Indeed, many classroom phenomena are so unexpected and their causes so hidden from sight that teachers tend to treat them as minor miracles. This attitude is particularly evident when the event in question is pedagogically desirable. When a student makes a sudden leap of progress or when an apathetic youngster undergoes a dramatic reversal of attitude, the teacher's response, quite naturally, is apt to be one of delight and thankfulness. But this response is unlikely to be followed by an analytic scrutiny of what has taken place. When good fortune strikes, the teachers seem to be saying, it is best not to ask too many questions.

The unquestioning acceptance of classroom miracles is part of a broader tendency that reveals itself in several ways in the talk of teachers. This is the tendency to approach educational affairs intuitively rather than rationally. When called on to justify their professional decisions, for example, my informants often declared that their classroom behavior was based more on impulse and feeling than on reflection and thought. In other words, they were more likely to defend themselves by pointing out that a particular course of action *felt* like the right thing to do, rather than by claiming that they *knew* it to be right. As the structure of a teaching session or of a class day unfolds, the teacher frequently behaves like a musician without a score. He ad-libs.

It must be remembered, of course, that the impulses and intuitive hunches of most of these teachers had been tempered by years of practical experience. Thus, the basis of their action might be much more rational than their self-reports would lead us to believe. In their daily doings they may, in effect, be rendering "by heart" a type of performance that would have to be carefully reasoned and rehearsed by a group of novices. But whether they advanced to this intuitive level late in their careers or whether they performed this way from the beginning is less important within the present context than is the fact that now, as seasoned teachers, they often reported themselves to be playing the melody by ear.

The alert critic will be quick to point out that almost all of the interviewees were women, thus intimating that the so-called intuitive quality revealed in the interviews is nothing more than interviewees exercising their feminine birthright. "After all," he might argue, "women are supposed to be intuitive. Why should we be surprised to find female teachers behaving like other women?" But the important question is not whether the teachers are more intuitive than their non-teaching sisters. Rather, it is whether they are unnecessarily intuitive when their actions might better be guided by reason. We must ask, in other words, about the overall propriety of intuition in the classroom. No one objects if a cook adds an extra pinch of salt just because she feels like it. But the same behavior on the part of a pharmacist is quite another matter.

One might expect people who do not inquire into the reasons for things and who tend to act impulsively to be indecisive when expressing their own tastes. But, judging from the interviews, classroom teachers could hardly be so described. Despite the weakness of their intellectual tenacity and the intuitive softness of their talk, they commonly expressed strong opinions concerning their ways of teaching. Moreover, the strength of their opinions did not seem to be affected by the fact that they were often unable to defend their choices. Like amateur art-lovers they knew what they liked, even if they did not always know why they liked it. When pressed for a rationalization of their pedagogical tastes they not infrequently became impatient or hid behind the defense of *de gustibus non est disputandum.* Rarely, if ever, did they turn to evidence beyond their own personal experience to justify their professional preferences.

A fourth indicator of the conceptual simplicity contained in the teachers' language is reflected in the narrowness of the working definitions they assign to common terms. Although teachers often use words and phrases denoting global aspects of human behavior (such as *motivation, social relations,* and *intellectual development*) the referents of these terms, on close inspection, are usually found to contain only pale reflections of the rich concepts from which they are derived. *Motivation,* in pedagogical shop-talk, typically refers to a student's zest for undertaking school assignments, and little else. *Social relations* commonly has as its sole referent the quality of the student's interaction with his classmates and his teacher, and the complexity of that definition is often further reduced to a crude estimate of the student's popularity with his peers. When intellectual development is discussed by teachers, that development is described almost exclusively in terms of the student's mastery of curricular objectives, or a summary statistic depicting his performance on a test of general ability. As might be expected, these conceptual curtailments correspond roughly to the limits of the teacher's experience in the classroom. Teachers do not usually have occasion to probe the unconscious motives of their students or sketch the contours of their social life space or examine the depths of their intellectual powers. Perhaps it is not surprising, therefore, to find that profound words, in the teachers lexicon, have a distinctly parochial cast.

The narrowness of the definitions assigned to global terms not only provides further evidence of conceptual simplicity, it also serves to introduce another major characteristic of teachers' language. Even though she may attach abstract labels to what she observes, the focus of the teacher's concern is on her concrete experience with a particular group of students. In brief, she lives in a world of *sharp existential boundaries* and those boundaries evince themselves in the way she talks.

There was a striking immediacy about the things that concerned the teachers—a here-and-nowness about their talk that becomes compellingly evident after prolonged listening. Perhaps this quality should not surprise us. After all, during every working day the teacher is immersed in an environment of real people and things whose demands upon her are continuous and insistent. Moreover, many of the unique features of her world become so well known to the teacher that it becomes difficult for her mentally to erase their identity and think of them as merely concrete manifestations of more abstract phenomena. Consequently, generalizations about the characteristics of children or about the merits of an educational theory are continually being tested, as the teacher considers them, against the qualities of the particular students with whom she is working and the specific constraints of her classroom. As might be expected, this degree of specificity greatly inhibits the easy translation of theory into practice and serves to increase the difficulty of communications between the teacher and others with more abstract interests.

The teacher's focus on the physical and social reality of her classroom—her embeddedness, so to speak, in the here-and-now—is not the only indicator of existential boundaries defining the limits of her concern. In addition, there are signs of emotional ties to her students and to other aspects of her environment, ties binding her even more securely than does mere familiarity to the setting in which she works. Of course everyone cares to some extent about what he is doing and about his daily associates. To that extent, then, teachers are no different from anyone else. But the intensity of the teacher's emotional investment in her work, if we can believe the way she talks about it, often exceeds this common concern. In this respect, teachers resemble clergymen, therapists, physicians, and others whose duties link them intimately to the personal well-being of their clientele. Yet the teacher's clientele, it must be remembered, are children and her contact with them is much more intensive in most cases than is true for those who perform these other professional services.

The teacher's concern with the here-and-now and her emotional attachment to her world was often accompanied in her conversations by an accepting attitude toward educational conditions as they presently exist. Interest in educational change was usually mild and typically was restricted to ideas about how to rearrange her room or how to regroup her students—how to work better with the educational "givens," in other words. Rarely, if ever, was there talk of the need for broad or dramatic educational reforms, even though the interviews provided ample opportunity to discuss these matters. This acceptance of the status quo, which might be described as a kind of pedagogical conservatism, appeared to be part of the general myopia typifying the classroom teacher's intellectual vision.

From one point of view, the features of teachers' language that have been described here are anything but flattering. Lacking a technical vocabulary, skimming the intellectual surface of the problems they encounter, fenced in, as it were, by the walls of their concrete experience, these teachers hardly look like the type of people who should be allowed to supervise the intellectual development of young children. Yet it must be remembered that most of the teachers from whose conversations these generalizations were derived were themselves highly respected practitioners of the teaching craft. Three possible explanations of this apparent paradox deserve brief comment.

First, it is possible that the evidence was badly misread. Perhaps someone else listening to the same set of interviews would come up with impressions quite different from those presented here. Second, it is possible that these teachers were not as highly gifted as their administrators and colleagues thought they were. Perhaps they more closely resemble the average, or even below-average, practitioner than they do the masters of their craft. Third, it is possible that the seemingly undesirable aspects of teachers' language are not so undesirable after all. Perhaps those qualities that might be a hindrance in many other settings do not adversely affect the teacher's functioning in the classroom. Indeed, it may even be that what looks like a general weakness in the quality of the teacher's thought processes is actually a strength when seen within the context of her life in the classroom.[5]

The possibility of having grossly misread the data or of having inadvertently chosen an inappropriate sample cannot be effectively

148

---

[5] The possibility of socially undesirable traits having adaptive significance for the teacher has also been suggested by J. M. Stephens in his fascinating article, "Spontaneous schooling and success in teaching," *School Review*,

dismissed. Consequently, it is necessary to remain skeptical while considering the third and far more intriguing possibility: namely, that what seems to be a human failing on the part of the teachers may be, at least in part, a pedagogical virtue.

The job of managing the activities of 25 or 30 children for 5 or 6 hours a day, 5 days a week, 40 weeks a year, is quite a bit different from what an abstract consideration of the learning process might lead us to believe. In the small but crowded world of the classroom, events come and go with astonishing rapidity. There is evidence, as we have seen, to show that the elementary school teacher typically engages in 200 or 300 interpersonal interchanges every hour of her working day. Moreover, although that number may remain fairly stable from hour to hour, the content and sequence of those interchanges cannot be predicted or preplanned with any exactitude. In short, classrooms are not neat and orderly places even though some educational theories make them sound as if they are or should be. This does not mean that there is no order in educational affairs (indeed, some teachers strive so hard to maintain some semblance of order that they lose sight of everything else), but the structure underlying these kaleidoscopic events is not easily discerned, nor is it, except superficially, under the control of the teacher.

149

The personal qualities enabling teachers to withstand the demands of classroom life have never been adequately described. But among those qualities is surely the ability to tolerate the enormous amount of ambiguity, unpredictability, and occasional chaos created each hour by 25 or 30 not-so-willing learners. What is here called the conceptual simplicity evident in teachers' language may be related to that ability. If teachers sought a more thorough understanding of their world, insisted on greater rationality in their actions, were completely open-minded in their consideration of pedagogical choices, and profound in their view of the human condition, they might well receive greater applause from intellectuals, but it is doubtful that they would perform with greater efficiency in the classroom. On the contrary, it is quite possible that such paragons of virtue, if they could be found to exist, would actually have a deuce of a time coping in any sustained way with a class of third graders or a play-yard full of nursery school tots.

The existential boundaries said to be revealed in the talk of teachers may also have adaptive significance when considered in the context of the demands of classroom life. There is a certain appropriateness, even charm perhaps, in the image of the absent-minded professor. If he is to do his work well he must be able, at

68:152–163, Summer 1960. This argument is more fully elaborated in his recent book, *The Process of Schooling: A Psychological Examination* (New York: Holt, Rinehart and Winston, 1967).

least figuratively, to free himself for long periods of time from his physical and social surroundings. But the image of an absent-minded elementary school teacher is not nearly so appealing. Indeed, such a combination of qualities might prove to be quite disastrous. People who work with groups of children cannot afford to be absent, in either mind or body, for any extended period of time. Moreover, even after the pupils leave for home they are gone but not forgotten in the mind of their teacher. The slightest mention of an abstract concept having educational overtones is enough to stir up a vision of Carl, the red-headed boy in the third row.

There is, of course, something romantic, even sentimental perhaps, about the image of teachers being presented here. But that romanticism is itself consonant with the qualities being described. Although they might never verbalize it in these terms, the interviewees, as a group, did seem to lean toward a tender-minded world view. Despite their immersion in the here-and-now, their view of children was definitely idealized and was tinged with a quasi-mystical faith in human perfectability. These signs of romantic idealism and mystical optimism may be disturbing to many people, especially to researchers and others who believe their mission in life is to dispel such old-fashioned views. But the persistence of this tender-mindedness in generations of teachers is surely no accident. Like conceptual simplicity and sharp existential boundaries, it too may have its adaptive significance. As Broudy and Palmer remind us in their informative book, *Exemplars of Teaching Method:*

> Modern psychology has given a solid and nonsentimental basis for mental hygiene and careful attention to child development, but unless a culture is entranced by the potentiality of childhood and passionately devoted to its realization, the commitment to the long nurture of the young would be prudential at best. Once the "cosmic" dimension of childhood is dropped, the life and activities of the child degenerate either into means to be manipulated for the benefit of adults or into a necessary but unfortunate marking of time.[6]

The teachers with whom I have spoken would probably agree with this statement, at least intuitively.

Here, then, are a few impressions stimulated by the talk of teachers. From one point of view, that talk does indeed leave much to be desired. It might even be described as dull much of the time. Yet, if listened to carefully and if considered in the light of what we know about classroom life, it does begin to make a lot of sense.

---

[6] Harry Broudy and John Palmer, *Exemplars of Teaching Method* (Skokie, Ill.: Rand McNally, 1965), p. 129.

VI

Sometimes teaching is described as a highly rational affair. Such descriptions often emphasize the decision-making function of the teacher, or liken his task to that of a problem-solver or hypothesis-tester. Yet the interviews with elementary teachers raise serious doubts about these ways of looking at the teaching process. The immediacy of classroom life, the fleeting and sometimes cryptic signs on which the teacher relies for determining his pedagogical moves and for evaluating the effectiveness of his actions call into question the appropriateness of using conventional models of rationality to depict the teacher's classroom behavior.

This questioning of the usefulness of rational models is not intended to imply that teaching is totally irrational or that the customary laws of cause and effect somehow fail to operate in the classroom. Obviously events are as lawful there as they are in any other sphere of human endeavor. But the activities assumed to accompany rational thought processes—activities such as the identification of alternative courses of action, the conscious deliberation over choice, the weighing of evidence, the evaluation of outcomes—these and other manifestations of orderly cognition are not very salient in the teacher's behavior as he flits back and forth from one student to another and from one activity to the next.

The fact that the teacher does not appear to be very analytic or deliberative in his moment-to-moment dealings with students should not obscure the fact that there *are* times when this is not true. During periods of solitude, in particular, before and after his face-to-face encounter with students, the teacher often seems to be engaged in a type of intellectual activity that has many of the formal properties of a problem-solving procedure. At such moments the teacher's work does look highly rational.

This brief mention of the teacher's behavior during moments when he is not actively engaged with students calls attention to an important division in the total set of teaching responsibilities. There is a crucial difference it would seem between what the teacher does when he is alone at his desk and what he does when his room fills up with students. Although this difference was not explicitly mentioned in the interviews with the elementary teachers it was implicit in their discussion of such matters as the relationship between lesson plans and their daily work. In the classroom, as elsewhere, the best laid schemes suffer their usual fate.

The distinction being made here between two aspects of the teacher's work is so fundamental and has so many implications for educational matters that it deserves some kind of official recognition in the language used to describe the teaching process. The terms "interactive" and "preactive" might serve this purpose. What the teacher does vis-à-vis students could be called "interactive teaching" and what he does at other times—in an empty classroom, so to speak—could be called "preactive teaching." These terms help us keep in mind a qualitative difference that is often overlooked in educational discussions.

There is something special, in a cognitive sense, about interactive teaching, about what goes on when a teacher is standing before his students. At such times the spontaneity and immediacy and irrationality of the teacher's behavior seem to be its most salient characteristics. At such times there appears to be a high degree of uncertainty, unpredictability, and even confusion about the events in the classroom.

At first glance the teacher's intuition, his delight over the mystery of human change, and his buoyant optimism appear strangely out of keeping with the highly organized setting in which he works. Such qualities might even be expected to be dysfunctional when they occur in a person who must perform within the confines of a formal institution. Highly rational and reality-oriented persons —tough-minded realists—might seem much better suited to the demands of the teaching task than are the tender-minded romantics who currently do the job. Yet this judgment of fit is not as easy to make as it first appears. As we look more closely at what goes on in an institution we begin to see how our present cadre of elementary school teachers, with all of their intellectual fuzziness and sticky sentimentality, may be doing the job better than would an army of human engineers.

One way in which the world view that has been discussed may be educationally beneficial is by prompting actions that serve as antidotes to the toxic qualities of institutional life. By being less than completely rational and methodical in his dealings with students the teacher may help to soften the impact of the impersonal institution. In a world of time schedules and objectives and tests and routines, the teacher's humanness, which includes his feelings of uncertainty and his Boy Scout idealism, stands out in bold relief.

Ideally, teachers might help to protect students in several ways from the anonymity and isolation implicit in institutional living. First, and most important, they come to know their students and to be known by them. Much of the teacher's effective knowledge as he goes about his work consists of idiosyncratic information about the particular set of students with whom he deals. Thus, the teacher may help to preserve the student's sense of personal identity by responding to him as a person, not just as a role incumbent.

Second, in some classrooms the teacher not only knows his

students as persons, he also *cares* about them. He takes delight in their progress and is disappointed by their failure. This empathic response to a student's progress, or lack of it, may of course be feigned rather than genuine. But even when students come to realize that teachers, like other adults, are sometimes merely being polite in their praise and sanctimonious in their reproof, it is doubtful that these actions lose all of their effect. As we all know, a favorite device of young children when dealing with competitive claims or threats from their peers is to respond with the query: "Who cares?" The answer to that question, when it refers to matters dealing with school and school work, is usually: "The teacher."

Another aspect of the teacher's caring about his students involves his missing them when they are not there. The individual student is much less indispensable to the operation of a classroom than is his teacher. Witness the practice of hiring substitutes for teachers but not for students. It is almost as if a student's presence in a room does not really matter except to the student himself. Teachers, however, frequently note absences and often comment on them. As a result students are encouraged to feel that their own presence or absence might make a difference after all.

A third, and for our purposes, final, way in which the teacher might help to dull the sharp edges of classroom life is by presenting his students with a model of human fallibility. Unlike the computer in the records office and the electrical system that regulates the bells and buzzers, classroom teachers sometimes get angry or laugh or make mistakes or look confused. Unlike televised instructors or teaching machines or textbooks, real live teachers must often confess (if they are honest) that they do not know something or that they have made an error. Thus teachers are able to personify the virtue of possessing knowledge while at the same time demonstrating the limits of that virtue. In this way the abstract goals of learning are given a human referent. Students cannot aspire to become a computer or a teaching machine or a textbook but they can aspire to become a teacher.

At this point some readers, searching their memories of past and present dealings with elementary school teachers, may complain that the image presented here is too idealized and partakes too much of the teacher's own tendency to romanticize his work. Many teachers, it might be argued, do not really care about their students, except in the most superficial way; many do not really miss their students when they are absent, except perhaps when the absentees are teacher's pets. Moreover, the fallibility of many teachers may be so great that rather than serving as a model of the attainable they personify instead the comic and the undesirable. Add to this the fact that many teachers act like obsequious handmaidens of school administrators and their function as human antidotes to institutional constraints begins to look like a sentimental pipe-dream.

Yet reality surely lies somewhere between the ideal and the cynical views of the teacher's function. What is more, each extreme can probably be found to exist in some classrooms. The important point is that the teacher has it within his power to dull some of the abrasive aspects of school life *if he so desires*. Moreover, certain qualities of the teacher's general outlook, his world view as it has been called here, seem like natural prerequisites for his serving to make classroom life more tolerable for students.

Clearly the teacher is not the only agent who might make the institutional aspect of school life easier to take. In most classrooms, particularly in the upper grades, there is also a well-established peer culture which is connected to activities outside the school and which operates internally to reduce discomfort, or to strengthen the student's resistance by sharing criticism, subverting regulations, ridiculing authority, and in other ways providing defenses against the more unpleasant aspects of institutional living. The student who suffers an injustice in the hands of his teacher or who chafes under the constraint of an unyielding rule can usually find solace among his peers.

But whether he gets it from his teacher or from his peers or elsewhere, the individual student often stands in need of protection, of a sort, from those qualities of classroom life that threaten his sense of uniqueness and personal worth. It is also likely that he needs this protection while he is physically present in the institution and that compensatory experiences at home or at play will not be adequate substitutes for a humane classroom environment. School comprises too large a segment of a child's life to have its effect completely neutralized by what happens after the dismissal bell rings.

Finally, this discussion reveals a fundamental ambiguity in the teacher's role. In a sense he is working for the school and against it at the same time. He has a dual allegiance—to the preservation of both the institution and the individuals who inhabit it. This double concern and the teacher's way of dealing with it imbues his work with a special quality. The social theorist Charles Horton Cooley, once pointed out that,

> An institution is a mature, specialized and comparatively rigid part of the social structure. It is made up of persons, but not of whole persons; each one enters into it with a trained and specialized part of himself . . . in antithesis to the institution, therefore, the person represents the wholeness and humanness of life. . . . A man is no man at all if he is merely

a piece of an institution; he must stand also for human nature, for the instinctive, the plastic and the ideal.[7]

Paraphrasing Cooley, we might conclude that a teacher is no teacher at all if he is merely a piece of an institution. He too must stand for qualities extending beyond the official boundaries of his task. Some teachers (no one seems to know how many) recognize this fact and act accordingly.

[7] Charles Horton Cooley, "Institutions and the person," in *Sociological Theory*, E. Borgatta and Henry J. Meyer (eds.), (New York: Knopf, 1956), p. 254.

The Need for New Perspectives **5**

The trivial helps reveal the sublime. . . .
Sometimes the things one calls little are big,
larger than they appear—or than one suspects.
Sometimes, with the passing of years, they turn
out to be enormous.

Walter Teller, "Thoughts and Days,"
The American Scholar, Winter 1966–1967

The thesis of this final chapter is that some of the sources to which educators have traditionally turned for guidance and advice are not likely to move the field of education as far forward as it was once believed they might. In particular, it will be argued that the understanding and tactics of the learning theorist and the human engineer are of less potential value to the practicing educator than is commonly assumed. Both of these perspectives fail in significant ways to come to grips with the reality of classroom events. It will also be argued that the perspective of the clinical-oriented psychologist, though clearly relevant to important aspects of the teacher's work, is of limited value in understanding much of what happens between the morning bell and dismissal. A new look at teaching, if there is to be one, seems to require us to move up close to the phenomena of the teacher's world. But such a move, though long overdue, is just the beginning.

I

From a common-sense viewpoint, the linkage between teaching and learning is so intimate—or appears to be—that an understanding of the one process would seem to imply an understanding of the other. If we knew all there was to know about learning we ought to know, or be able to deduce, all there is to know about teaching. At least, so it would seem. This expectation, in one form or another, has enjoyed widespread popularity among psychologists and educators alike. It has bolstered the hope that a scientific theory of learning will be developed which will have immediate and direct consequences for the improvement of the teacher's work.

But, as every classroom teacher knows, this hope has not yet been fulfilled. Despite a half century of research and the development of several sophisticated theories, the teacher's classroom activities have been relatively unaffected by what the learning theorist has to say. There have been several notable efforts to identify the implications of various learning theories for teaching practice. But usually these implications contain little more than common-sense advice hardly requiring for their persuasiveness the scientific efforts of the learning theorist (for example, "children must be motivated in order to learn"). The work of B. F. Skinner, which may ultimately have a noticeable impact on education through the development of the teaching machine movement, is a possible exception to this overall state of affairs, but the fact remains that teachers, even in these days of programmed instruction, are largely ignorant of what the learning theorists are up to. Moreover, despite the seemingly logical link between teaching and learning, teachers do not seem to be suffering from their ignorance.

The failure of learning theory to transform the teacher's work has been widely discussed in educational and psychological circles. Several alternative explanations have been offered to account for it. One view is that the learning theorist's knowledge is not easily extrapolated to human affairs because it is based largely on the study of rats and other lower forms of life. Humans, so the argument goes, are more complex than are rats or other animals and, thus, their behavior obeys a different set of laws than those designed to account for the learning of other species.

Another explanation, closely related to the one involving species differences, focuses on differences in the complexity of learning tasks. According to this view, the learning theorist's knowledge applies chiefly to the acquisition of simple skills and the attainment of artificial objectives. Many educators would insist that such knowledge has little to say about skills and understandings that are complex and personally meaningful to the learner. Critics developing this argument would stress the fact that even when human subjects are used in laboratory experiments they commonly are presented with tasks or with learning objectives that are contrived and meaningless.

A third way of explaining the limited applicability of learning theory to the teacher's work is by calling attention to the differences between the controlled environment of the laboratory and the more or less chaotic conditions under which learning normally occurs. In his search for regularities in behavior the experimenter seeks to eliminate, or at least to control, extraneous influences. As a result, he typically observes phenomena under *un*natural conditions. The teacher, in contrast to the researcher, has relatively little control over many of the variables impinging upon his work. Thus, a set of learning principles that does not hold under the conditions of everyday life is of limited usefulness to him.

These three explanations have in common the contrast between the complexity of the teacher's work and the simplicity of the conditions under which much of our formal learning theory has been generated. In his choice of subjects, in the level of learning objectives, and in the structure of the experimental setting, the learning theorist introduces conditions that place severe limits, though scientifically defensible ones, on the applicability of his findings to the practical business of classroom teaching. Although these are the explanations most commonly introduced when discussing the contribution of learning theory to educational practice, they are not the only ones that could be mentioned. Two other possibilities, though less obvious that the three already discussed, seem at least equally deserving of attention.

The complexity of the teacher's work extends beyond the fact that he is concerned with a complex organism, working toward complex goals, in a complex setting. He also, in most instances, is working with a *group* of students. The social character of the classroom adds yet another dimension to the teacher's work and further accounts for his limited reliance on learning theory when seeking pedagogical advice.

The learning theorist typically works with one subject at a time. Rarely, if ever, does he train a flock of pigeons to peck at a target, or a pack of rats to press a bar. In short, he behaves more like a private tutor than like a classroom teacher. This way of working is understandable, of course, given his research goals. But the findings obtained in such a context are of limited relevance to a teacher who is in charge of twenty or thirty students. Like the researcher, the teacher also works with individual subjects from time to time but even during such moments (and they are much less frequent than the educator's talk of individualized instruction would have us believe) he is usually mindful of the presence of others and adapts his behavior accordingly. When he is trying to sustain a group discussion, or introducing a new unit, or demonstrating a skill, or overseeing a committee's work, or proctoring an examination, the teacher is deeply immersed in the social network of the room. At such moments (and such moments are frequent in most classrooms) the teacher's knowledge of learning theory is an unlikely source of help.

This brief description of the social character of the teacher's work sets the stage for an even more serious question regarding the relationship between teaching and learning. As we think of the total range of the teacher's activities and the amount of time he spends doing various things, we are led to wonder whether the teacher's *primary* concern is learning, after all. If substantiated, this possibility, which almost sounds heretical, would go even further toward explaining the educator's apparent disinterest in formal theories of learning than have the views already put forward.

The separation of teaching and learning, even in the interest of intellectual speculation, is likely to arouse protests from professionals and laymen alike. If the teacher is not chiefly concerned with learning, with what is he concerned? Surely no one could quarrel with the proposition that the major, perhaps even the only, purpose of teaching is to promote learning. Even allowing for the fact that teachers often have to perform noninstructional duties such as collecting the milk money or taking attendance, or ordering supplies, the heart of their work, or so it would seem, is the guidance of students from a state of ignorance toward greater knowledge. And if that is not learning, the critic might ask, what is?

The problem turns, it would seem, on the distinction between the teacher's *primary* concern and his *ultimate* concern, on the thoughts and practices dominating his immediate actions with students, as contrasted with his hopes and expectations concerning the long-term achievement of individuals within his class. Teachers, particularly in the lower grades, seem to be more activity-oriented than learning-oriented. That is, they commonly decide on a set of activities which they believe will have a desirable outcome and then focus their energies on achieving and maintaining student involvement in those activities. Learning is important, to be sure, but when the teacher is actually interacting with his students it is at the periphery of his attention, rather than at the focus of his vision.

In the interactive setting the teacher commonly encourages his students to do what he thinks will be good for them without giving too much thought to the precise outcome of his instructional efforts. At first glance this lack of precision might appear to be a pedagogical shortcoming, and indeed it is criticized as such by proponents of so-called behavioral objectives (about which more will be said later), but an analysis of some of the qualities of classroom life already examined in this volume does much to dispel such hasty criticism. Considering only the numerical facts, so to speak—the number of hours spent in school, the number of students in each room, and the number of subjects in the curriculum—the teacher's imprecision in establishing goals becomes understandable, if not forgiveable.

In some ways, the teacher's concern with the learning of his students is similar to a mother's concern with the nutrition of her children. Most mothers surely desire their children to develop healthy and strong bodies and they understand the general relationship between the quality of food they provide and the status of their child's health. But in planning their meals the nutritional value of the foods they use is thought of, if at all, in the very broadest terms. Many other variables, such as cost, convenience, esthetic quality, and idiosyncratic taste play a part in the selection and preparation of the family diet. Because of the adaptiveness of humans, in most cases the result is a healthy family.

Like mothers, teachers have responsibility for definite aspects of their students' growth. They too understand the overall relationship between their daily activities and the achievement of educational ends. But in their moment-by-moment decisions the details of this relationship, the process of learning per se, is not uppermost in their minds. Rather, they seem to be guided by certain rule-of-thumb considerations that are constantly being modified by the specifics of each classroom situation. The result, if we can believe achievement test scores and other indicators of academic attainment, is "normal" educational growth for most students.

This comparison of the work of parents and teachers might be easily misinterpreted as an apology for the status quo or as a defense of pedagogical sloppiness. Neither is intended. There is no reason to believe that teaching cannot be better than it presently is, nor is there any evidence that sloppiness is any more tolerable in the classroom than in the kitchen or in the doctor's office. Rather, the point is simply that teachers are only indirectly concerned with the details of the learning process, even though a vague understanding of that process may be found to underlie their immediate actions. As they have developed to date, most learning theories contain more information about the learning process than the average teacher wants, or needs, to know.

II

From time to time in the field of education there emerges a movement designed to modernize the institutional operations of the schools by bringing them into closer harmony with the spirit that guides the development of technology in industry, government, and the applied sciences. The forces behind these cyclic efforts are ill-defined and more often seem to arise from the prevailing climate of opinion than to be instigated by any identifiable persons or groups. One such effort in the late twenties and early thirties was referred to as "the scientific movement in education" and flourished for several years before being eclipsed by the forces of progressivism. At present we seem to be in the midst of another such effort, this time referred to (at least in the popular press) as "the technological revolution in education."

Although labels are dangerous, particularly when applied to such diverse phenomena as those under discussion, many of the forces at work to change today's schools and the practices of today's teachers seem to be best described as representing an "engineering" point of view. Such a descriptive label, though admittedly inaccurate, helps us to focus on a scattered set of influences and pressures that promise to transform the teacher's work. Whether the overall impact of such forces will be beneficial or detrimental is not within the scope of this discussion. It is within its scope, however, to examine some of the limits of an engineering viewpoint as applied to classroom affairs.

The elements contained in such a viewpoint consist, essentially, of a set of values and a group of educational procedures by which those values might be implemented. Sometimes the values are spoken of explicitly and are openly defended; at other times they are implicit and are assumed to be imperatives, "givens," about which no one could seriously argue. Both the values and their supporting methodology combine to form a moral perspective from which to view specific educational problems and practices.

The core of values to be discussed here—the "goods," so to speak, of the engineering point of view—comprise the standards by which one might judge a piece of machinery or the plans for achieving a military objective. The first question, of course, is: will it work? will it get the job done? This question, which entails the criterion of effectiveness, implies a clear idea of what job is to be done or what objectives are to be reached. Next comes a series of secondary questions having to do with the efficiency of the procedure under consideration. After ascertaining that it will work, the critic is next interested in knowing whether it will do so speedily, accurately, precisely, and economically. These questions are chiefly concerned with the conservation of energy and expense. In the best of all possible worlds, according to this view, jobs should be done as cheaply and as quickly as possible, with a minimum amount of wasted motion.

When these criteria are applied to educational affairs they encourage the teacher, first, to be as precise as possible in stating his teaching objectives. Preferably these objectives should be couched in "behavioral terms," because only then, so the argument goes, can the teacher tell when he has reached them. The job of determining how close he is to his objectives is the second piece of educational advice implicitly contained in the criterion of effectiveness. The teacher is admonished not only to pin-point his destination but also to chart his course, as it were, by taking periodic readings that will tell him how far he is from his goal. Finally, the teacher and his students are implicitly advised not to dawdle along the way. So long as the teacher is certain about what he wants to do and how to do it, nothing is to be gained by moving more slowly than is necessary or by consuming more energy than the task requires.

Here then, in capsule form, is a set of recommendations that have had unusual force in educational discussions over the past twenty or thirty years. They have given impetus to the educational testing movement, have guided curriculum theory, and currently undergird the renewed interest in educational technology. In the view of many educational leaders the improvement of teaching depends almost solely on the willingness of larger numbers of teachers to heed these pedagogical canons and behave accordingly. The result, it is claimed, will be the transformation of teaching from an art to a science.

There is no denying the logical appeal of this point of view. Nor can there be any doubt about the educational benefits that have accrued from acting on it. The objective testing movement has already been cited as one such outcome. Many improvements in textbooks and curricular materials are further outgrowths of the same methodological position. Given these substantial contributions it would be foolish to call into question the overall merits of what is here being called the engineering point of view.

Yet it is reasonable to ask whether there are any limits to this way of thinking about educational matters. How precise in the definition of his objectives and in the evaluation of his students' progress can or should the classroom teacher become? Are the concepts of wasted motion and inefficiency as useful in the design of new educational activities as they are in the design of a new auto engine? Are there aspects of classroom life that are not amenable to analysis in these terms? Questions such as these are of extreme importance as we move toward a better understanding of school life. For no matter how powerful the engineering point of view might be, its usefulness is limited if, under its influence, we are dissuaded even momentarily from examining the total spectrum of classroom events.

The major weakness of the engineering point of view as a way of looking at the teaching process is that it begins with an over-simplified image of what goes on in elementary school classrooms. The business of teaching involves much more than defining curricular objectives and moving toward them with dispatch; and even that limited aspect of the teacher's work is far more complicated in reality than an abstract description of the process would have it seem. When it is remembered that the average teacher is in charge of the twenty-five or thirty students of varying abilities and backgrounds for approximately 1000 hours a year and that his responsibilities extend over four or five major curricular areas, it is difficult to see how he could be very precise about where he is going and how to get there during each instructional moment. He may have a vague notion of what he hopes to achieve, but it is unreasonable to expect him to sustain an alert awareness of how each of his students is progressing toward each of a dozen or so curricular objectives.

This point is similar to one of the explanations of why teachers do not rely on learning theory to guide their actions. And the similarity deserves emphasis because it concerns a basic condition of the teacher's work, a condition that helps to explain why many of the fruits of research and theoretical speculation remain undevoured, as it were, by practicing educators. At the simplest level it seems the teacher is just too busy to be bothered with the intellectual and pedagogical frills of learning theory and precisely defined objectives. Faced with twenty or thirty restless students he has enough to do without worrying about whether his behavior is in accord with the pronouncements of the theorists or the admonishments of the curriculum planners.

This description of the teacher's plight is accurate so far as it goes, but it does not go far enough. It implies that if only there were some extra hours in the day or if only classrooms contained fewer students, teachers would then behave as external critics of the teaching process say they should. But the problem is not just that the teacher is too busy, although that is surely part of it. It is also that he is engaged in a process that is qualitatively unlike the descriptions implied in learning theories and in what is here called the engineering view of educational progress.

As typically conducted, teaching is an opportunistic process. That is to say, neither the teacher nor his students can predict with any certainty exactly what will happen next. Plans are forever going awry and unexpected opportunities for the attainment of educational goals are constantly emerging. The seasoned teacher seizes upon these opportunities and uses them to his and his student's advantage. If a discussion is moving along at full tilt he may decide to forget about a scheduled test and let the discussion continue. If a student makes an unusual error in his arithmetic workbook, he may call the class to attention and warn them against making a similar mistake. If a fight breaks out on the playground, the teacher may decide to cancel the activity planned for the next period and spend the time talking to his students about the meaning of fair play. And so it goes. Although most teachers make plans in advance, they are aware as they make them of the likelihood of change.

Although gross changes in the teacher's plans provide the clearest evidence of the unpredictability of classroom events, the same quality is also revealed through a more microscopic analysis of teacher-pupil interaction. Stray thoughts, sudden insights, meandering digressions, irrelevant asides, and other minor disruptions constantly ruffle the smoothness of the instructional dialogue. Experienced teachers accept this state of affairs and come to look upon surprise and uncertainty as natural features of their environment. They know, or come to know, that the path of educational progress more closely resembles the flight of a butterfly than the flight of a bullet. Moreover, if we believe the kind of testimony presented in the last chapter, the majority of teachers seem to enjoy working under these conditions and actually look forward to having their plans spoiled by the occurrence of unexpected events.

The uncertainties of classroom life are not limited to the unexpected events occurring there but also include the complicated contingencies that bear upon many, if not most of the teacher's decisions. When he has to decide, as an instance, whether to call in the parents of a student who is having difficulty, the relevant considerations include not just the student's progress or lack of it, but also some estimate of how the parents will respond to this action, how this might affect the student's perception of his teacher, how other students will react to the episode, and so on. When he is trying to decide whether to continue with a unit on the American Indians or move to a new topic in social studies, the relevant considerations include not just how much the students know about Indians but also some estimate of their level of interest, the number of topics to be covered by the end of the year, the relationship between the social studies and other curricular areas, and so on. Even in the minutae of the teacher's behavior this complexity is present, though perhaps not so evident. When, for example, he is in the act of deciding which student to call on from among those with raised hands, he often thinks in a twinkling about which student was called on last, which one has not yet made a contribution, which one is most likely to give the right answer, which one needs to be shaken out of a state of lethargy, and so on. 167

These examples of the complexity of the teacher's decisions are not offered to impress the reader with the difficulty of the teaching task, although they may have that effect as well. Rather, they are intended to illustrate an inevitable quality of the teacher's work, a quality that places severe limits on the usefulness of a highly rational model for describing what the teacher does. Given the complexity of his work, the teacher must learn to tolerate a high degree of uncertainty and ambiguity. He must be content with doing not what he *knows* is right, but what he *thinks* or *feels* is the most appropriate action in a particular situation. In short, he must play it by ear.

When teachers look back upon a day's activities and ponder the wisdom of their actions, the criteria they apply to what they have done are not limited to the achievement of educational objectives. They also worry about whether they were just or unjust in the distribution of praise and reproof, sensitive or insensitive to the nuances of the events that transpired, consistent or inconsistent in the standards and regulations they enforced. They are interested, in other words, in stylistic qualities of their own performance as much as in whether specific goals were reached and specific objectives attained. At such moments the engineering virtues of speed, efficiency, accuracy, and economy are not uppermost in their minds.

The teacher's unwillingness or inability to be precise in the statement of "behavioral" objectives is sometimes cited as evidence of his lack of objectivity. The alternative to talking in behavioral terms, so the argument goes, is to talk in a subjective language that has little relation to what goes on in the real world. In part, this criticism is justified. Many teachers doubtlessly do give insufficient attention to the effect they are trying to achieve. But in another sense, teachers are more behaviorally oriented than they are given credit for being. As the teacher keeps his eye out for signs of restlessness and inattention, as he learns to discriminate between feigned and genuine involvement in a learning activity, his concern for concrete behavior is fully as great as that advocated by the proponents of behavioral objectives. Languid postures, drooping eyelids, averted gazes—these are signs that things are not going as they should in the classroom, whereas alert expressions, waving hands, and frowns of concentration are signs that things are going as they should. Teachers learn how to interpret this language of classroom behavior and adjust their instructional procedures accordingly. In so doing, they are about as closely attuned to the real world as they can be.

Finally, the complaint that school is a waste of time occurs frequently enough to give some credence to those who insist upon greater speed, economy and efficiency in educational affairs. Perhaps the teacher's characteristic lack of concern about such matters is indeed a major weakness in our present system. But the charge of wasted time, if it is to be taken seriously, must be examined more closely than is customarily done. Only then does its educational significance become clear.

Time can be wasted in at least three ways: by doing something more slowly than is necessary, by having nothing to do when activity is desired, and by doing something that turns out later to have been unnecessary or futile. It is also possible, of course, to feel that time is being wasted when it actually is not, and, conversely, to feel that time is not being wasted when it actually is. When these varieties of wasted time and their accompanying feelings are considered within the context of classroom affairs, the simple charge that school is a waste of time takes on additional complexity.

In terms of subjective discomfort, the least painful form of wasting time is that in which the movement toward a goal is slower than it need be. So long as progress of any sort is evident the situation is likely to be tolerable although it might surely arouse feelings of impatience. A slowly moving line of cars on an expressway provides a good example of a situation in which this form of discomfort is commonly experienced. When the traffic comes to a complete halt, however, there is usually a noticeable rise in the level of psychic stress. Now horns begin to blow and tempers mount. But the most debilitating experience of all occurs when the trip turns out to have been in vain or when the traveler is convinced of its futility from the start.

These common situations in which most of us have found our- selves from time to time have their analogues in classroom affairs. Students can have a sense of moving along more slowly than is necessary, they can find themselves with nothing to do during moments when they want to be doing something, and they can fail to understand, with or without justification, the significance of what they are doing. Under all three of these circumstances they are apt to feel that time is being wasted. But from a psychological standpoint the feelings aroused under the first set of circumstances are not likely to be as devastating as are those aroused under the other two conditions.

When we consider the classroom conditions likely responsible for these three types of subjective experience, it becomes apparent that considerations of speed, economy, and efficiency in education focus our attention on only one possible cause of wasted time in the classroom, and in some sense on the least important cause. It is true that if students could master material more rapidly they presumably could master more material, but it is doubtful that such an improvement, in and of itself, would markedly decrease their sense of wasting time in the classroom.

Several features of classroom life that might contribute to the "wasted-time syndrome" have been discussed throughout this book. They include the countless interruptions and petty delays, the ubiquitous lines that clog the halls, the compulsory nature of school attendance, the ever-present anticipation of future pleasures. These features, as we have seen, arise from the institutional character of the school and the size of its population. So long as students have to wait around, whether it be to make a contribution to the group discussion or to take their turn at the teaching machine, the experience is likely to engender some sense of wasted time.

But, as every teacher knows, the problem of eliminating a feeling of wasted time extends beyond keeping students busy and avoiding unnecessary delays. It includes convincing them that the compulsory activities are worthwhile after all and that the things they are busy at are not just "busy work." This conviction, which depends ulti- mately on the teacher's own faith in what he is doing, would prob- ably be more time-saving, in a psychological sense, than would any number of instructional short-cuts.

III

Another source to which teachers have turned for help is the expertise possessed by the clinically-oriented psychologist or the mental health expert. Logically at least, from such persons would seem to flow great insight into the problems teachers typically face. If the learning theorist and the engineer are too impersonal in their concerns, the clinician is surely the antithesis of that point of view and, accordingly, should have no end of advice to give the teacher who must continually deal with situations involving real people.

In an overall sense, the educational benefits of the mental health perspective cannot be denied. As teachers have become more sensitive to the psychological underpinnings of their task much of the old-fashioned harshness and cruelty of classroom life have disappeared. Although critics might make fun of educators' talk about "meeting the needs" of children, there can be little doubt that such talk, which grows out of the wholistic approach characterizing the mental health movement, has a salutary effect on educational practices.

Despite these benefits, however, there are limits to how far the mental health perspective can take the teacher toward understanding the complexities of his task. These limits derive, in large measure, from several important differences between the concerns of clinicians and those of teachers. Although there is appreciable commonality in these two sets of concerns, the overlap is far from perfect.

A chief difference between the clinician and the teacher is that the former is principally concerned with pathology, whereas the latter is principally concerned with normality. For the teacher, pathological behavior, when it occurs, introduces a disruptive element in his work; something that must be overcome, so to speak, if he is to get on with his proper business. For the therapist, such behavior is the *raison d'être* of his professional activity. Admittedly, the distinction between the pathological and the normal is not always easy to make. It might even be argued that all so-called normal behavior contains pathological elements. But even allowing for the ambiguities involved in such a distinction, the mental set with which the teacher customarily views his students is quite different from the therapist's view of his patients. This difference may only be relative, but it is nonetheless real. If the teacher were totally to adopt the clinician's view he would be led to concentrate on issues that are commonly at the periphery of his concern.

Paralleling the relative emphasis on the pathological and the normal is a difference in the degree to which teachers and clinicians attend the intellectual and the emotional aspects of behavior. Again, there is no way of sharply distinguishing these two spheres of human functioning and, consequently, both teachers and therapists must maintain a dual interest in how people think and in how they feel. But the teacher's unique responsibility is to equip his students to deal skillfully with their social, ideological, and physical surroundings. Accordingly, he is more concerned than is the therapist with the total spectrum of human competence. This concern also carries with it an evaluative perspective that is missing or only slightly evident in the therapist's view.

Clinicians sometimes talk about the therapeutic value of "unconditional positive regard" or some other nonevaluative stance which they attempt to maintain in their relationships with their clients. A few have advocated that teachers adopt a similar posture in their dealings with students. No doubt many teachers are unnecessarily harsh in their evaluative practices and, hence, could benefit from the clinician's advice. But given the teacher's responsibility for guiding intellectual growth, there are limits to the extent to which he can maintain a nonevaluative atmosphere in the classroom. As many teachers will testify, it is rather difficult to communicate unconditional positive regard while informing a student that all of the arithmetic problems he completed that morning were done incorrectly. No doubt a skillful teacher can reject an incorrect answer without rejecting the child who gave it, but no matter how much he values his students unconditionally he cannot abrogate his role as a judge of academic performance.

The teacher's allegiance to the individual is almost always tempered by his allegiance to the class as a whole and the tension created by this dual focus represents yet another difference between his work and that of the clinician. Like the learning theorist, the clinically-oriented psychologist typically deals with one person at a time (group therapists being the obvious exceptions). As a result, he has relatively little to offer the teacher who frequently must tend to the plight of an individual student while keeping his eye on a roomful of others. Therapy rarely takes place under crowded conditions; teaching commonly does.

Another missing component in the clinician's view, from the standpoint of its usefulness to the teacher, is an appreciation of how the immediate social setting gives shape and meaning to human behavior. As every teacher knows, a student's actions are grossly controlled by the constraints and the opportunities existing within the classroom. The same behavior in a different context would not necessarily have the same meaning. Indeed, from the teacher's viewpoint the *appropriateness* of the student's actions to the conditions under which they occur—the degree to which the behavior "fits" its context, so to speak—is of primary concern. Clinicians, by and large, do not fully share this environmental focus. Rather, they tend to be more interested than are teachers in a contextfree assessment of the individual.

From a clinical perspective the central "causes" of behavior reside within the individual. A person does what he does, in this view, because of interests, needs, motives, values, and other internal motivational structures. Therefore, to understand behavior, the argument continues, it is necessary to reveal these hidden springs of action. Moreover, if we want to change behavior significantly we must concentrate on detailed procedures for altering this intra-psychic world. The ephemeral push of the outside world is weak when compared with the enduring thrust of these internal dynamics. Or so it would seem when life is viewed from a therapist's vantage point.

But the view of behavior gained from standing in front of a class is of quite a different order. From the teacher's perspective much of the behavior he witnesses seems to be "caused" not by some set of mysterious driving forces hidden within his students but by his own actions as a teacher. If he tells his students to take out their spelling books, the spelling books appear, if he asks a question, hands go up, if he calls for silence, he usually gets it. In other words, many obvious and dramatic shifts in students' behavior are largely under his control. This is not to say that his students are merely marionettes who twitch on command. Even though most students comply with his requests there are always a few who do not. Unpredictable and unexplainable events, as we have seen, are the teacher's constant companions. But for the most part, classrooms, like churches and cafeterias, are such highly structured and coercive environments that the observer does not need a detailed knowledge of the internal states of the participants in order to understand what is going on there. Motives, interests, needs, and other psychic mechanisms surely affect behavior in these settings but the influence of these idiosyn-cratic motivational structures is greatly tempered and restrained by situational demands. The clarification and management of these demands make up a central part of the teacher's work. As he seeks ways of trying to do his job better, the teacher who turns to an intensive study of personality dynamics or psychological pathology may discover that he has learned more about alligators than he needs to know.

Beneath the surface of classroom events lies the complex world of individual psychology. At times it is imperative for the teacher to enter that world. On such occasions he is forced to pause and try to unravel the psychic entanglements that accompany the unusual educational performance of individual students. But it is unfeasible, given the range of his responsibilities, for him to pause too long or too often. Of necessity, therefore, his psychological knowledge of most of the students under his charge will remain superficial from a clinician's point of view. And so it must be.

The important question is whether a superficial view, from a clinical perspective, can be an adequate view in an educational sense. In other words, would knowing more about each and every student really help the teacher perform more effectively? One approach to this question is to ask whether it is necessary for the teacher to know anything about his students. When asked in this extreme form the answer is obviously "yes." Clearly the teacher is better able to plan for his class after he has been with them for a while than he is on the first day of school. But it is also probably true that there is some point of diminishing returns beyond which increased knowledge no longer adds to the teacher's proficiency.

An understanding of how such limits might operate requires that we distinguish between the *how* and the *why* of human behavior. Typically, teachers are more interested in how a student reacts to certain educational experiences than in why he behaves the way he does. Billy, they discover, is a hard worker who can be counted on to complete the tasks assigned him and to ask for more. John, by way of contrast, tends to dawdle and "wastes" his time during seat-work, although he is an active participant in group discussions. Sarah, who is a whiz in reading and who likes to stay after school to help the teacher, seems to be listless and disinterested during science class. Maxine, the most popular girl in the room, excels in art and can be counted on to handle responsibility conscientiously. And so it goes. For each child, as the year progresses, the teacher develops a more or less adequate understanding of how he behaves in recurring educational situations. Though doubtless this information is more extensive and more accurate for some students than for others, in combination it comprises the teacher's image of the educational givens with which he must work.

The importance of understanding why students behave the way they do depends, in part, on the behavior in question. As the teacher considers a student's strengths, for example, the 'why' question is almost pedagogically irrelevant. Who cares why Billy is such a hard worker, or why John comes to life in a group discussion, or why Maxine is so good in art? The truth, whether clinicians like it or not, is that most teachers are more thankful than inquisitive about these positive conditions.

The origins of educational deficiencies are clearly more relevant to the teacher's work than are the origins of desirable behavior because, presumably, the teacher might want to do something to change these states of affairs. But, as every clinician knows, the teasing out of these causal antecedents can be a long and tedious process under the best of conditions. Moreover, even if the roots of these behaviors could be easily revealed, the benefit of such knowledge to the teacher would still be questionable. So what if Sarah's distaste for science stems from a poor experience she had in the previous grade rather than from a basic dislike for her father who is a scientist? What difference would these two explanations have for the teacher's treatment of Sarah? The answer, quite bluntly, is: precious little.

Sarah's teacher has the job of teaching science (and social studies, and reading, and spelling, and math, and more) to 25 or 30 students three or four times a week. The best he can do under these circumstances is to make the subject as interesting as possible, to encourage Sarah whenever the opportunity affords itself, and to hope for the best. If Sarah moves out of her anti-science mood before June, the teacher, quite naturally, will be delighted. But if she moves on to the next grade with a continuing distaste for all things scientific, the teacher can hardly accept this condition as evidence of professional failure.

Teachers are interested in individual students, to be sure. They worry about them as they watch their behavior in class and they may even carry their worries to the office of the school psychologist. The help the teacher receives while there may sensitize him to the psychological drama that lies just beneath the surface of his daily work. More particularly, it may provide him with a deeper understanding of those few students who pose serious pedagogical problems. Such help is indeed an important contribution to the teacher's overall effectiveness.

But even with this help, his task, as a teacher, is not lightened significantly. The problem student will probably continue to be a problem despite the teacher's newly gained understanding. And even if he does not, the bulk of the teacher's burden remains. For teaching involves much more than trying to figure out how to deal with the few students who excite the interest of the clinician. It involves deciding which text to use in reading and how to spark up the new social studies project and what to do about the progress reports due next week. It includes worrying about the new seating arrangements and the science table that never seems to be used and the workbooks that need to be checked. Concerning issues such as these, and, indeed, concerning most of the issues that make his job complex, the teacher's clinically-oriented advisors can do little more than shrug their shoulders.

IV

People who are interested in the application of learning theory or the engineering point of view to teaching practice often have as their goal the transformation of teaching from something crudely resembling an art to something crudely resembling a science. But there is no good evidence to suggest that such a transformation is either possible or desirable. An equally reasonable goal, and one more in keeping with the views expressed in this book, is to seek an understanding of the teaching process as it is commonly performed before making an effort to change it. As we learn more about what goes on in these densely populated hives of educational activity it may turn out that we will seek to preserve, rather than to transform, whatever amount of artistry is contained in the teacher's work.

The goal of discovering what really goes on in classrooms is certainly not new, even though it could hardly be called the dominant concern of today's educational researchers. Much is already known about how to set out in pursuit of such a goal and we also have a fair idea of some of the sights to be encountered along the way. It may be gratuitous, therefore, to end a book such as this with either admonishment or advice concerning how future work might proceed. Yet a few such statements do seem in order, if only because the point of view represented here is still far from enjoying wide acceptance in most educational circles.

First, it almost goes without saying that in the future more researchers will spend more time observing in more classrooms, or at least poring over records of classroom events. There has already been a noticeable increase of observational studies in recent years and the trend looks as though it will continue.[1] Moreover, there is some evidence that classroom researchers are beginning to turn to disciplines other than psychology and educational measurement for their methods of analyzing classroom phenomena.[2] The techniques of participant observation and anthropological field study are among those receiving greater attention from educational researchers.

But though much can likely be gained by increasing the number of participant observers in our schools, the growth in our understanding of what goes on in these environments need not be limited to the information contained in the field notes of professional teacher-watchers. In addition to participant observers it might be wise to foster the growth of observant participators in our schools—teachers,

---

[1] The work of Marie Hughes, B. O. Smith, Ned Flanders, Jacob Kounin, Arno Bellack, Edmund Amidon, and Hilda Taba is representative of this trend.
[2] The recent studies of Louis Smith, Bruce Biddle, and Jules Henry make use of some of these newer methodologies.

administrators, and perhaps even students, who have the capacity to step back from their own experiences, view them analytically, and talk about them articulately.[3] It is probable that only a few participants will ever be equipped, by either temperament or training to do this job while continuing to perform their regular duties, but considering the size of our teaching population even one out of every ten thousand or so teachers would be sufficient to comprise a salient group of "internal critics" of the teaching process.

If observational studies of classrooms increase, new ways of talking about teaching are also bound to emerge. It is doubtful, however, that these different descriptive languages will readily congeal into anything like a unified theory of teaching. Instead, we are likely to see the emergence of several critical perspectives from which to view classroom events. Each perspective, it may be hoped, will provide the practitioner and the researcher with a unique strategy of inquiry with which to examine educational affairs. In the work described in this book, for example, the focus has been on the institutional matrix in which teachers and students are embedded. Such a perspective, if successful, should lead teachers and others to ask questions about the school's operation that they might not otherwise have asked.

It should be noted in passing that the descriptive terms derived from observational studies may provide a language of educational criticism that will be useful to insiders and outsiders alike. When teachers and researchers begin to talk the same language, as it were, the possible benefits that each may derive from listening to the other will be greatly increased. At present teachers in particular lack an effective set of descriptive terms for talking about what they do. As a result, they often must fall back on clichés and outworn slogans when called upon to describe their work. Perhaps such a state of affairs is inevitable. Perhaps by the time a set of critical terms has become common among teachers it has already hardened into clichés. But the need for a fresh and vibrant language with which to talk about educational affairs seems apparent.

Almost as important as observation per se is the requirement of keeping an open mind about what we see. Our ways of looking at the classroom should not be unnecessarily restricted by prior assumptions about what should be going on there, nor even, as we have seen, by the seemingly logical link between the abstract processes of teaching and learning. In short, we must be prepared and willing to give up many of our comfortable beliefs about what classroom life is all about.

---

[3] The recent writings of John Holt offer a striking example of the insights to be gained from articulate practitioners.

Finally, as we look we must keep in mind the ubiquity of classroom phenomena in both time and space. Only as we remember that each classroom minute is one of millions of similar minutes experienced by millions of persons and by each person millions of times, are we led to look closely at the details of the events before us. Considered singly many aspects of classroom life look trivial. And, in a sense, they are. It is only when their cumulative occurrence is considered that the realization of their full importance begins to emerge. Thus, in addition to looking at the dominant features of instructional interchanges and the overall design of the curriculum we must not fail to ponder, as we watch, the significance of things that come and go in a twinkling—things like a student's yawn or a teacher's frown. Such transitory events may contain more information about classroom life than might appear at first glance.

Intended as a stimulus to thought about education problems, this is a classroom-oriented description of the elementary school teaching-learning process in which the school is examined as a setting for human activity.

The book was written with one significant feature of a child's early life in mind: institutional membership. Adults spend most of their waking hours coping with the demands of institutional life, and school is where it all begins. Professor Jackson emphasizes the early years of schooling, for it is during this period that the young child comes to grips with the facts of institutional life. During these formative years the child develops adaptive strategies that will stay with him throughout the balance of his education and beyond.

The school's abrasive qualities as a social institution are considered at length. The